SpringerBriefs in Law

SpringerBriefs present concise summaries of cutting-edge research and practical applications across a wide spectrum of fields. Featuring compact volumes of 50 to 125 pages, the series covers a range of content from professional to academic. Typical topics might include:

- A timely report of state-of-the art analytical techniques
- A bridge between new research results, as published in journal articles, and a contextual literature review
- A snapshot of a hot or emerging topic
- A presentation of core concepts that students must understand in order to make independent contributions

SpringerBriefs in Law showcase emerging theory, empirical research, and practical application in Law from a global author community. SpringerBriefs are characterized by fast, global electronic dissemination, standard publishing contracts, standardized manuscript preparation and formatting guidelines, and expedited production schedules.

Emma J. Scaife

Urban Tree Protection on Private Land

A Review of Regulatory Mechanisms in Australia

Springer

Emma J. Scaife
School of Agriculture and Environment
University of Western Australia
Crawley, WA, Australia

ISSN 2192-855X ISSN 2192-8568 (electronic)
SpringerBriefs in Law
ISBN 978-981-95-1856-2 ISBN 978-981-95-1857-9 (eBook)
https://doi.org/10.1007/978-981-95-1857-9

This Springer imprint is published by the registered company Springer Nature Singapore Pte Ltd.
The registered company address is: 152 Beach Road, #21-01/04 Gateway East, Singapore 189721, Singapore

For my mum, Jacqueline, who brought me to the trees.

Foreword

Most of us are well aware of the importance of protecting natural habitats for the health and survival of plants and animals, even if we often act as if the resources of the planet are inexhaustible and we exaggerate the capacity of living things to bounce back from any adversity. But we pay less attention to the effect of such environmental degradation on *us* and what it implies for the planning of our cities and neighbourhoods, although it is clear that the quality of the natural environment affects our health and our general well-being, and not just via its physical effects.

There is mounting evidence confirming the beneficial effects for people, especially children, of having "contact with nature" and of detrimental outcomes when the natural environment is degraded. Indeed, the Intergovernmental Platform on Biodiversity and Ecosystem Services identified nature's contributions to people as one of the key elements in the relationship between humans and the natural world. This understanding informed their recommendation that such relationships should be a routine part of decision making about infrastructure and land use; that non-material benefits from the natural world—well-being, aesthetics, leisure, recreation and identity—need to be central, not peripheral considerations.

The strong body of evidence derived from research in many disciplines that living in green space is particularly beneficial to people's health and well-being produces a long list, worth collating: reduced stress, better sleep, improved mental health, reduced depression and anxiety, greater happiness, well-being and life satisfaction, reduced aggression, reduced ADHD symptoms, increased pro-social behaviour and social connectedness, lower blood pressure, improved postoperative recovery, birth outcomes and pain control, improved child development (cognitive and motor), reduced congestive heart failure, reduced obesity and diabetes, better eyesight, improved immune function, improved general health, and reduced mortality. The findings of benefit are compelling, not least because they are derived from a wide variety of approaches, methods and places.

A steady stream of such findings led the WHO to recommend that "urban green space is a necessary component for delivering healthy, sustainable and liveable cities. Interventions to increase or improve urban green space can deliver positive health, social and environmental outcomes for all population groups, particularly among lower socioeconomic status groups. There are very few, if any, other public health interventions that can achieve all of this, and especially the impact on active lifestyles, mental well-being and social interaction is frequently highlighted as a key benefit".[1]

At the same time as evidence mounts of the importance of the natural world to human well-being, we are steadily, inexorably and knowingly stripping our cities and towns of tree canopy, mostly in the service of new housing developments and bigger houses, built boundary to boundary. Much of this destruction is occurring on private lands, while governments at all levels appear helpless to stem the loss. We can celebrate the efforts of local heroes attempting—sometimes successfully—to defeat the chainsaws and grinders in their precious local places, but we know that the scale of the destruction requires more systemic and concerted effort.

Without the legal tools, monitoring and enforcement mechanisms, little will be achieved. In this book, Emma Scaife provides some much-needed analysis and policy research, recognising that "With insufficient public land to support canopy cover goals, and tree loss on private land continuing unabated, governments' urban canopy targets are practically impossible to achieve: private land is the key to improving canopy cover in Australian cities." She has meticulously and extensively canvassed the extent and source of the problem and evaluated the various legal and administrative tools currently in use to protect trees and urban greenspace in private lands throughout Australia. As she clearly illustrates, understanding the cultural, economic, and political constraints on any proposed actions is rudimentary. Importantly, her diagnosis of the problems and shortcomings of various regulatory mechanisms and policies at all levels of government is followed by evidence-based suggestions about alternative approaches and remedies which might prove more successful in reversing the decline of urban forest on private land.

This is a very timely and welcome contribution to improving our vital urban green space; to give more weight to the quality of our lives and the collective benefits of greening our suburbs.

Perth, Australia Carmen Lawrence

[1] WHO, Urban Green Space Interventions and Health: A review of impacts and effectiveness, p 5, A4 Colour cover, vernacular.

Acknowledgements This work was created on Whadjuk Noongar country. It was completed as part of a Ph.D. undertaken at The University of Western Australia and is supported by an Australian Government Research Training Program (RTP) Scholarship.

I am grateful for the wise guidance and input from my Ph.D. supervisory team: Associate Professor Ram Pandit, Professor Emeritus Alex Gardner and Dr. Stephen Willey. Dr. Willey in particular was tasked with devoting considerable attention to the first draft of each chapter of this book, a task which no doubt seemed interminable as chapter drafts kept appearing month after month. I also wish to humbly thank Professor Emeritus Carmen Lawrence AO, the Chair of my Ph.D. Advisory Panel, for her invaluable counsel throughout the progress of this project and for very kindly agreeing to write the Foreword. Finally, I extend my thanks to my husband Michael, who has been a great support for me during this endeavour, not least by providing endless cups of tea.

Although every effort has been made to ensure this manuscript is error-free, any remaining mistakes and errors are mine. If any are spotted by a diligent reader, please do let me know.

Competing Interests The author has no competing interests to declare that are relevant to the content of this manuscript.

Contents

About the Author

Emma J. Scaife holds a Bachelor of Laws (UWA) and a Master of Environmental Management (ECU). She worked as a lawyer in Perth, as a senior associate for top tier law firms in Melbourne and London, and led a policy team for the British Government introducing new legislation in the UK. More recently, Emma has focused on environmental causes, volunteering at The Woodland Trust (UK) and the Environmental Defenders Office (WA). In 2015, Emma received the Bluebell Award for Best Guardian of Woods and Trees for her work with the Woodland Trust. In addition to her current research on urban forest regulation with the University of Western Australia, Emma is also the founder and co-ordinator of an environmental advocacy program for Nature Conservation Margaret River Region.

Chapter 1
Introduction

Abstract Globally, the human population is increasingly residing in urban areas, and it is predicted that by 2050, 68% of the global population will live in cities. As cities expand and densify, they often do so at the expense of trees and forests. This trend contributes to the global environmental problems of climate change, biodiversity loss and land use change. Urban trees and forests have a valuable role in mitigating these environmental issues, as well as providing a suite of other benefits to urban communities. As governments realise these benefits, strategies are being devised to support and increase urban trees and forests. In Australia, urban canopy cover is increasing on public land, but continuing to decline on private land. This short book reviews the existing regulatory mechanisms which are relevant to protecting and increasing urban trees and forests on private land in Australia. It covers research, legislation and case law relevant to each mechanism and includes discussions of research on the effectiveness (or otherwise) of these mechanisms in reversing the decline of urban forest on private land.

1.1 Trees and Cities

1.1.1 Urbanisation

Globally, the human population is increasingly residing in urban areas, and the United Nations' Population Division predicts that by 2050, 68% of the global population will live in cities [1]. In Australia, the urbanisation pattern is ahead of global predictions: the urban population has increased from 58% of the total population in 1911 to 90% in 2021 [2]. Australia is a highly urbanised nation.

Australia has also experienced significant population growth, increasing from 3.8 million in 1901 to 25.7 million in 2021 [2]. Population growth, together with urbanisation, have led to the ongoing expansion and densification of Australian cities [3].

E. J. Scaife, *Urban Tree Protection on Private Land*,
SpringerBriefs in Law, https://doi.org/10.1007/978-981-95-1857-9_1

Fig. 1.1 Photograph of commemorative paving stone in Perth, Western Australia. Photograph by Scaife, E., 2024

As cities expand and densify, they often do so at the expense of trees and forests. In Australia, in the early- to mid-1800s, the initial creation of a town or city was declared by the felling of a tree [4] (Fig. 1.1).

According to the Australian Government's State of the Environment Report released in 2021, the potential environmental pressures from greater urban expansion in Australia include land clearing, reduced canopy cover and fewer gardens [3].

1.1.2 Benefits and Disservices of Urban Trees

1.1.2.1 Benefits

It is well established that urban trees and forests have a valuable role in mitigation of environmental impacts from climate change and in supporting biodiversity, as well as providing a suite of other environmental and health benefits to urban residents. The multiple benefits of urban trees include:

- carbon removal and storage [5–7]
- creating a cooling effect (of approximately 1 °C for every 10% increase in canopy cover) that can mitigate the urban heat island effect [8, 9]
- emissions reduction by promoting active transport and reducing vehicle use [5], and by cooling buildings thus reducing the use of air conditioners [10–12]
- water regulation and purification by reducing stormwater runoff and filtering pollutants [13–15]
- air purification by reducing air-borne pollutant concentrations [16, 17]
- biodiversity support by providing food and habitat for wildlife and reducing landscape fragmentation [18, 19]
- improving physical health by, for example, being linked to better immune system health and cardiovascular function [20–22]
- improving mental well-being by, for example, improving cognition and social cohesion, and reducing anxiety [22–24]
- reducing crime [22, 25]
- providing wind breaks [26]

- reducing unwanted noise (such as traffic noise) [27, 28]
- providing privacy screening between neighbours [29]
- reducing the impact of extreme weather events such as cyclones [30]
- providing wood for use as fuel [29]
- providing a food source; beautification (a key reason cited for landowners planting trees on private land) [29]
- increasing property values[1] [31, 32].

Most benefits have been found to vary in their level of impact depending upon factors such as the location, species, density of planting, and the size and health of the tree. Some benefits also vary depending on the season, or the time of day. Benefits are also often linked to each other. For example, one study found links between urban green space, cooler temperatures and reduced outdoor crime in Sydney [25]. Another study found the use of trees as wind breaks could amplify the cooling and air purification benefits obtained from urban trees [26].

1.1.2.2 Disservices

Urban trees also present a number of potential disservices, including: leaf litter; damage to buildings and infrastructure from roots or branches; allergic reactions; hosting pests; and safety risks from dropping limbs or trees falling [33, 34]. There are also carbon emissions and irrigated water use associated with tree maintenance activities, and potential stored carbon release at the end of a tree's life (depending on the disposal method) [33]. Trees can also block light, decreasing solar access for renewable energy [35], and can block desirable views. There is evidence that trees can increase air pollution in some circumstances by preventing pollution dispersal [36]. The higher property values that can be associated with urban trees may also cause residents to be displaced due to increased rents or houses becoming less affordable. This 'green gentrification' effect is a potential negative impact of urban trees [37].

As with benefits, most disservices will vary in their level of impact depending upon factors such as the location, species, size and health of the tree. Some authors have commented that disservices are largely ignored by many authors and professionals when considering the benefits of urban trees, and that failure to consider the disservices can lead to unintended negative consequences in decision-making about urban trees [33, 38, 39].

---

[1] Higher property values are not always viewed as a benefit, since this can lead to increased rents and less affordable housing.

1.2 Australian Government and Land Use Systems

Australia is a federated nation with three tiers of government. The Federal or Commonwealth Government is the central government, established by the Constitution of Australia in 1901. There are six states (New South Wales, Queensland, South Australia, Tasmania, Victoria and Western Australia) and two self-governing territories (Northern Territory and Australian Capital Territory). These comprise the second tier of government, are independent of each other and hold most powers and responsibilities. The third tier of government is local government. There are over 500 local governments (or local councils) within Australia, with certain powers and responsibilities granted by the relevant state and territory governments. Each local government's powers are limited to a specified local government area (LGA).

State parliaments may make laws on any subject matter, including any environmental issues. The Commonwealth Parliament's legislative powers are limited to a list specified subject matters, which may indirectly authorise the making of laws about environmental issues. Thus, environmental matters are the subject of concurrent powers of both the Commonwealth and state / territory governments. For example, the Commonwealth Government may make treaties creating Australia's international obligations, and the Commonwealth and state / territory parliaments may legislate to implement those obligations. However, to the extent that there is any conflict between concurrent laws of the Commonwealth and any state or territory law, those of the Commonwealth prevail. Australia's international obligations are the responsibility of the Commonwealth Government. Certain international obligations are potentially relevant to urban tree protection in Australia, and these are discussed in the following section.

Most legislation for land use, planning and building control is enacted by the states and territories, and typically confers local land use and building control powers on local governments, except where the land is held by the Commonwealth. State and territory legislation for regional land use and natural resources management typically confers regulatory powers on state and territory governments. At present, most Australian laws relevant to urban tree protection are made as part of planning or land use laws and regulations, and are the domain of state, territory or local government. Many local governments have also created local laws governing certain development and land use matters. There is no overarching requirement for consistency across Australia between all these laws for different jurisdictions, and consequently there is considerable variation in the definitions, standards and requirements on land use and planning matters. This has been criticised for creating a legislative patchwork effect and, with it, the lack of capacity to address Australia's international obligations on urban sustainability with a consistent approach [40].

1.3 Australia's International Obligations

1.3.1 Climate Change

Australia is a United Nations Member State and is party to a number of binding international agreements on climate change, including: the United Nations Framework Convention on Climate Change (in force for Australia from 1994) and the Paris Agreement [41] (in force for Australia from 2016) [42]. These agreements include obligations for reduction of greenhouse gas emissions. Although urban trees and canopy cover can assist in carbon sequestration and storage, the carbon carrying capacity of trees and forests is better utilised on a much larger scale than that available in urban areas. In Australia, most emissions reduction goals relevant to urban areas focus on building energy use and construction practices [40]. The use of trees to reduce energy consumption by naturally cooling buildings (and parked cars) sometimes feature as a part of programs across all levels of government for emissions reduction goals.

Climate change resilience and adaptation also form part of the international climate change action agendas. In addition, Australia has agreed to the Sendai Framework for Disaster Risk Reduction 2015–2030. As Australia's population is highly urbanised, climate related impacts and disasters in urban areas have the potential to impact disproportionately large numbers of people. In Australia, the key potential impacts for urban areas relate to coastal erosion, flooding, urban heat islands and reduced rainfall. Trees in urban areas can improve resilience to all of these impacts, and tree planting programs are increasingly being initiated as a nature-based solution for these types of issues, particularly by local governments. Fire, particularly bushfire, is also a disaster risk for many areas of Australia. Although more relevant to regional areas than urban locations, the regulations around management of bushfire risk typically also apply to urban areas and are often inconsistent with the regulated retention of trees and native vegetation. At present, regulatory controls imposed by local and state/territory governments tend to favour bushfire risk reduction over tree retention.

1.3.2 Biological Diversity

Australia has been a party to the Convention on Biological Diversity [43] since 1993. All parties to the Convention on Biological Diversity have adopted the 2022 Kunming-Montreal Global Biodiversity Framework [44]. The Framework includes 23 global targets for 2030, of which Target 12 addresses improving the area, quality and connectivity of green and blue spaces across urban areas. In accordance with these international biodiversity commitments, Australia has established a National Biodiversity Strategy, the current version of which is in Australia's Strategy for Nature 2024–2030 [45]. This strategy refers to a shared goal between Australian jurisdictions to halt and reverse biodiversity loss by 2030 and includes an objective to enrich cities and towns with nature (Objective 9), which specifically refers to increasing canopy cover in urban areas as a way of working towards this objective.

Australia's national law on biodiversity protection is the *Environment Protection and Biodiversity Conservation Act* (1999) (EPBC Act). It provides for a range of management and protection measures for plants and animals, with specific protection in Commonwealth areas and cooperative measures with the states and territories outside Commonwealth areas. For example, the measures include the listing of threatened species and ecological communities and permit protection of individual members of such species or communities in Commonwealth areas. Outside Commonwealth areas, the Commonwealth may cooperate with the states or territories in management planning. However, actions that will or are likely to have a significant impact on a listed threatened species or community require referral to the Commonwealth Minister administering the EPBC Act for a decision on whether the action needs an environmental impact assessment and approval. Australia also has a Threatened Species Action Plan 2022–2032, which includes targets of preventing new extinctions and conserving 30% of Australia's land area by 2032.

1.3.3 Sustainable Urban Development

1.3.3.1 The Earth Summit and Agenda 21

In 1992 the United Nations Conference on Environment and Development (known as the Earth Summit) held in Rio de Janeiro resulted in the Declaration on Environment and Development (agreed principles), and Agenda 21 (a non-binding action plan), broadly addressing the integration of environmental considerations into global development [46]. Agenda 21 (Chapter 11, in the context of combating desertification) addresses the need for the conservation and sustainable management of forests of all types. The urban forest is specifically included, by a call to stimulate urban forestry for protecting trees, and for amenity, recreation and production purposes [46].

1.3.3.2 Sustainable Development Goals

In 2015, Australia endorsed the non-binding 2030 Agenda for Sustainable Development, which included the 17 Sustainable Development Goals (SDGs). Globally, increasing trees and canopy cover in urban areas is seen as an efficient and cost-effective solution to help advance several of the SDGs [47, 48]. In particular, urban forests are relevant to: SDG 1 (No Poverty); SDG 2 (Zero Hunger); SDG 3 (Good Health and Wellbeing); SDG 6 (Clean Water and Sanitation); SDG 7 (Affordable and Clean Energy); SDG 8 (Decent Work and Economic Growth); SDG 11 (Sustainable Cities and Communities); SDG 13 (Climate Action); and SDG 15 (Life on Land) [48].

1.3.3.3 New Urban Agenda

The New Urban Agenda was adopted, including by Australia, at the United Nations Conference on Housing and Sustainable Urban Development (Habitat III) in 2016 [49]. The New Urban Agenda is a binding international commitment that has clear links with SDG 11 (Sustainable Cities and Communities). The New Urban Agenda comprises three core principles, the third of which relates to environmental sustainability in urban development:

> Ensure environmental sustainability by promoting clean energy and sustainable use of land and resources in urban development, by protecting ecosystems and biodiversity, including adopting healthy lifestyles in harmony with nature, by promoting sustainable consumption and production patterns, by building urban resilience, by reducing disaster risks and by mitigating and adapting to climate change. [49, p 8]

The core principles are supported by a number of formal commitments, which include specific commitments potentially relevant to urban trees; for example, green public spaces and gardens (Commitment 37); healthy societies (Commitment 55); improving urban ecosystems (Commitment 64); sustainable use of natural resources (Commitment 65); green networks (Commitment 67); and to prevent and contain urban sprawl, and prevent unnecessary land use change (Commitment 69) [49].

A literature review conducted in 2019 found that, apart from three Australian conferences held in the initial years following the adoption of the New Urban Agenda, there is little mention in literature of Australian governments' implementation of the New Urban Agenda [50]. In 2024, the Commonwealth Government prepared a draft National Urban Policy to replace a previous version prepared in 2011 [51] and outline 'the Australian Government's goals and objectives to enable our urban areas to be liveable, equitable, productive, sustainable and resilient' [51]. The draft Policy document refers to several of the SDGs and (albeit briefly) to the draft Policy's alignment with Australia's New Urban Agenda commitments [52].

1.3.4 Health

Australia has been a member of the World Health Organisation (WHO) since its establishment in 1948. The WHO has produced a number of reports about the health benefits associated with urban green spaces. The most recent report focuses on methods of valuing the contribution of urban green spaces to human health [53]. These WHO documents are informational and not binding on WHO members. In Australia, the health system is a shared responsibility between all levels of government, with states and territories having the most significant role. Utilising green spaces as a method of addressing health issues therefore tends to be a state or territory concern by choice, rather than a Commonwealth objective based on an international obligation.

1.4 Canopy Cover Statistics in Australia

1.4.1 Canopy Cover Mapping and Targets

The technological capacity to map and measure canopy cover and other vegetation in urban areas has undergone rapid development in the past two decades. Supported by Australian urban mapping developments such as CSIRO's Urban Monitor [54], local governments have been able to measure and track the canopy and urban forest cover in their LGA. In recent years there has been a proliferation of urban forest strategies and policies developed by state and local government bodies across Australia (for example, *Better Urban Forest Planning: A guide to support the enhancement of urban forests in Western Australia* [55]). These strategies typically include or recommend the setting of targets for increasing canopy or urban forest cover.

There is no set target for canopy cover that applies to all urban areas. Internationally the '3-30-300' rule is often referred to as a starting point. This is an evidence-based guideline suggesting that three trees should be visible from every home, a minimum of 30% canopy should occupy every neighbourhood and every resident should be within 300 m of a park or green space [56].

Many urban local governments have set canopy targets by reference to a percentage of cover to be achieved by a particular year. Some have refined the canopy cover percentages to be different for different land uses. A Perth study has tested a novel method for setting an optimal canopy cover target using input factors related to the specific benefits of urban trees relevant to the area covered [57].

1.4.2 Benchmarking Canopy Cover

As part of an initiative by Horticulture Australia to increase urban canopy cover (known as 'Greener Spaces, Better Places'), a project was undertaken in 2013 to provide a benchmark of canopy cover across Australian urban LGAs using iTree software [58]. The rationale for carrying out this benchmarking exercise was to motivate local governments to increase green infrastructure as part of sustainable development aims [58]. The results were summarised in a well-publicised guide entitled '*Where are all the trees?*' [59]. The project measured canopy, shrub, grass and hard cover across 139 LGAs (to broadly cover LGAs with urban areas). The initial results showed a national average of 39% canopy cover, although in later reports this was amended to 26.8% after applying a more accurate averaging method [60, 61]. Across all LGAs the canopy cover range was 3% to 79%, but the higher range was noted as potentially misleading because some of the LGAs that were assessed as having high tree canopy cover included extensive forested perimeter areas which accounted for a considerable proportion of the overall canopy cover.

Following up the original Greener Spaces Better Places benchmarking report, two further Australia-wide studies were undertaken to show trends in urban canopy cover

over time. These were the subject of reports in 2017 and 2020 respectively [60, 61]. In 2017, the national average canopy cover had dropped to 24.6% and by 2020 it was recorded slightly higher at 26.6%.[2] Nationally, between 2013 and 2020, there was an overall drop in green space (trees and shrubs) of 3.81% and an increase in hard surface cover of 3.83%. This benchmarking series demonstrated that Australian urban areas may be slowly increasing canopy cover from 2017, but by 2020 had not yet returned to pre-2013 canopy cover levels. It also showed that urban areas are continuing to lose overall urban forest cover in favour of hard surfaces [60].

The 2020 report included a survey of the views of local government staff on the challenges involved in attempting to increase canopy cover, with most reporting that limited and ineffective efforts relating to canopy cover on private land were the critical problem [60].

1.4.3 The Role of Private Urban Land

Private land is an important component of urban forest strategies, because privately-owned land makes up approximately 63% of all Australian land [62] and more than 80% of Australian land parcels in urban areas [63]. Due to the challenges involved with introducing laws and policies that may interfere with private property rights, it is also the most difficult component to regulate. Australia has a private property system based on common law principles which regard private property rights as fundamental. In 1948, the Universal Declaration of Human Rights stated: 'No one shall be arbitrarily deprived of his property' and in Australia, the High Court has confirmed that statutory laws will be read in favour of an interpretation which interferes least with private property rights [64]. Although there are many laws regulating the use and development of private land in Australia, these are typically justified as being necessary and in the public interest. Laws seen as interfering with private property rights are often challenged in the courts, particularly where there is a potential impact on the value of the property.

As part of the 2020 canopy benchmarking study noted above, survey data was obtained from local government professionals about the challenges in increasing urban forest cover, with most staff reporting:

> Despite challenges on private land, most recognise this is a critical area for improvement, but feel that state policy frameworks around land management do not support urban forest protection/enhancement on private land. [60, p 4]

The problem of improving tree retention and tree planting on private urban land appears as a general theme in several recent studies on urban forests [65–68]. This problem is significant, because privately-owned land makes up most of Australian urban areas [62] which means that declining urban forest on private land easily

---

[2] The final report used different percentages for canopy cover and shrubs in the 2013 benchmark, possibly due to excluding eight LGAs to match the lower number of LGAs reviewed in the later reports.

undermines canopy improvements on public land. This undermining effect is then reflected in overall urban canopy measurements. A recent study modelling canopy cover growth on public urban land in Melbourne concluded that there is insufficient public land for local governments to achieve their canopy cover targets and concluded that increasing canopy cover on private land needed to be part of the solution [69]. Similarly, a study modelling canopy cover for a new Sydney precinct found that most scenarios were unable to reach a canopy cover target of 40%, highlighting the need for canopy cover planning to extend to private land [70].

1.5 Scope of This Book

With insufficient public land to support canopy cover goals, and tree loss on private land continuing unabated, governments' urban canopy targets are practically impossible to achieve: private land is the key to increasing canopy cover in Australian cities. It is therefore important to understand the current mechanisms for regulation of trees on private urban land that are (or can be) used by local and state governments, and to examine the available literature on the effectiveness of those mechanisms [60, 71]. This book sets out to deliver this understanding, in a holistic way, going beyond the protection of existing trees to include mechanisms that influence the cycle of growth or decline of the urban forest over time.

This book does not cover topics that largely fall outside the scope of regulation relevant to improving overall canopy cover on private urban land. Excluded topics include neighbour disputes over trees, trees on public land, trees on non-urban land, and Indigenous or other cultural heritage laws applying to trees. Although this work includes examination of case law and legislation as appropriate, it is not written as, nor intended to be, a legal reference book and it does not comprise legal advice.

References

1. United Nations (2019) World Urbanization Prospects: The 2018 Revision (ST/ESA/SER.A/420). New York
2. Australian Bureau of Statistics (2021) Historical population. In: ABS Website. https://www.abs.gov.au/statistics/people/population/historical-population/latest-release. Accessed 22 Sep 2024
3. Cresswell ID, Janke T, Johnston EL (2021) Australia state of the environment 2021: Overview. Independent report to the Australian Government Minister for the Environment. Canberra
4. Appleyard RT, Manford T (1979) The beginning : European discovery and early settlement of Swan River, Western Australia. University of Western Australia Press for the Education Committee of the 150th Anniversary Celebrations, Nedlands, Western Australia
5. Fan L, Wang J, Han D et al (2022) Research on promoting carbon sequestration of urban green space distribution characteristics and planting design models in Xi'an. Sustainability 15:572. https://doi.org/10.3390/su15010572

6. Strohbach MW, Arnold E, Haase D (2012) The carbon footprint of urban green space—a life cycle approach. Landsc Urban Plan 104:220–229. https://doi.org/10.1016/j.landurbplan.2011.10.013
7. Ghosh S, Yung SH (2017) Carbon and economic benefits of urban trees in two Sydney transport corridor case studies. In: Ecocity World Summit 2017. Melbourne, Australia, pp 1–12
8. Yenneti K, Ding L, Prasad D et al (2020) Urban overheating and cooling potential in Australia: An evidence-based review. Climate 8:126. https://doi.org/10.3390/cli8110126
9. Brown H, Proust K, Newell B, et al (2018) Cool communities—urban density, trees, and health. Int J Environ Res Public Health 15. https://doi.org/10.3390/ijerph15071547
10. Rouhollahi M, Whaley D, Behrend M et al (2022) The role of residential tree arrangement: A scoping review of energy efficiency in temperate to subtropical climate zones. Renew Sustain Energy Rev 158:112155. https://doi.org/10.1016/j.rser.2022.112155
11. Rouhollahi M, Whaley D, Byrne J, Boland J (2022) Potential residential tree arrangement to optimise dwelling energy efficiency. Energy Build 261:111962. https://doi.org/10.1016/j.enbuild.2022.111962
12. Rouhollahi M, Behrend M, Boland J (2024) Optimising tree arrangement policy in Australian small-scale residential settings. Sustain Cities Soc 102:105232. https://doi.org/10.1016/j.scs.2024.105232
13. Grey V, Livesley SJ, Fletcher TD, Szota C (2018) Tree pits to help mitigate runoff in dense urban areas. J Hydrol (Amst) 565:400–410. https://doi.org/10.1016/j.jhydrol.2018.08.038
14. Berland A, Shiflett SA, Shuster WD et al (2017) The role of trees in urban stormwater management. Landsc Urban Plan 162:167–177. https://doi.org/10.1016/j.landurbplan.2017.02.017
15. Yang L, Zhang L, Li Y, Wu S (2015) Water-related ecosystem services provided by urban green space: A case study in Yixing City (China). Landsc Urban Plan 136:40–51. https://doi.org/10.1016/j.landurbplan.2014.11.016
16. Diener A, Mudu P (2021) How can vegetation protect us from air pollution? A critical review on green spaces' mitigation abilities for air-borne particles from a public health perspective—with implications for urban planning. Sci Total Environ 796:148605. https://doi.org/10.1016/j.scitotenv.2021.148605
17. Vieira J, Matos P, Mexia T et al (2018) Green spaces are not all the same for the provision of air purification and climate regulation services: The case of urban parks. Environ Res 160:306–313. https://doi.org/10.1016/j.envres.2017.10.006
18. Stagoll K, Lindenmayer DB, Knight E et al (2012) Large trees are keystone structures in urban parks. Conserv Lett 5:115–122. https://doi.org/10.1111/j.1755-263X.2011.00216.x
19. Manning AD, Gibbons P, Lindenmayer DB (2009) Scattered trees: a complementary strategy for facilitating adaptive responses to climate change in modified landscapes? J Appl Ecol 46:915–919. https://doi.org/10.1111/j.1365-2664.2009.01657.x
20. Browning MHEM, Rigolon A, McAnirlin O, Yoon H (Violet) (2022) Where greenspace matters most: A systematic review of urbanicity, greenspace, and physical health. Landsc Urban Plan 217:104233. https://doi.org/10.1016/j.landurbplan.2021.104233
21. Kondo M, Fluehr J, McKeon T, Branas C (2018) Urban green space and its impact on human health. Int J Environ Res Public Health 15:445. https://doi.org/10.3390/ijerph15030445
22. Wolf KL, Lam ST, McKeen JK et al (2020) Urban trees and human health: A scoping review. Int J Environ Res Public Health 17:4371. https://doi.org/10.3390/ijerph17124371
23. Astell-Burt T, Feng X (2019) Association of urban green space with mental health and general health among adults in Australia. JAMA Netw Open 2:e198209. https://doi.org/10.1001/jamanetworkopen.2019.8209
24. Navarrete-Hernandez P, Laffan K (2023) The impact of small-scale green infrastructure on the affective wellbeing associated with urban sites. Sci Rep 13:9687. https://doi.org/10.1038/s41598-023-35804-2
25. Stevens HR, Graham PL, Beggs PJ, Ossola A (2024) Associations between violent crime inside and outside, air temperature, urban heat island magnitude and urban green space. Int J Biometeorol 68:661–673. https://doi.org/10.1007/s00484-023-02613-1

26. Al-Obaidi I, Rayburg S, Półrolniczak M, Neave M (2021) Assessing the impact of wind conditions on urban heat islands in large Australian cities. J Ecol Eng 22:1–15. https://doi.org/10.12911/22998993/142967
27. Nourmohammadi Z, Lilasathapornkit T, Ashfaq M et al (2021) Mapping urban environmental performance with emerging data sources: A case of urban greenery and traffic noise in Sydney, Australia. Sustainability 13:605. https://doi.org/10.3390/su13020605
28. Cook D, Van Haverbeke D (1971) Trees and shrubs for noise abatement. Nebraska Agricultural Experiment Station: Historical Research Bulletins (Research Bulletin No 246)
29. Kirkpatrick JB, Davison A, Daniels GD (2012) Resident attitudes towards trees influence the planting and removal of different types of trees in eastern Australian cities. Landsc Urban Plan 107:147–158. https://doi.org/10.1016/j.landurbplan.2012.05.015
30. Van der Sommen FJ, Pearson DM, Boggs GS (2018) Analysis of the interrelationship between houses, trees and damage in a cyclone affected city: Can landscape design and planning utilising trees minimise cyclone impact? International Journal of Disaster Risk Reduction 28:701–710. https://doi.org/10.1016/j.ijdrr.2018.01.031
31. Pandit R, Polyakov M, Tapsuwan S, Moran T (2013) The effect of street trees on property value in Perth, Western Australia. Landsc Urban Plan 110:134–142. https://doi.org/10.1016/j.landurbplan.2012.11.001
32. Bottero M, Caprioli C, Foth M, et al (2022) Urban parks, value uplift and green gentrification: An application of the spatial hedonic model in the city of Brisbane. Urban For Urban Green 74. https://doi.org/10.1016/j.ufug.2022.127618
33. Roman LA, Conway TM, Eisenman TS et al (2021) Beyond 'trees are good': Disservices, management costs, and tradeoffs in urban forestry. Ambio 50:615–630. https://doi.org/10.1007/s13280-020-01396-8
34. Drew-Smythe JJ, Davila YC, McLean CM, et al (2023) Community perceptions of ecosystem services and disservices linked to urban tree plantings. Urban For Urban Green 82. https://doi.org/10.1016/j.ufug.2023.127870
35. Ko Y (2014) The effect of urban trees on residential solar energy potential. J Korean Inst Landsc Arch 42:41–49. https://doi.org/10.9715/KILA.2014.42.1.041
36. Grylls T, van Reeuwijk M (2022) How trees affect urban air quality: It depends on the source. Atmos Environ 290:119275. https://doi.org/10.1016/j.atmosenv.2022.119275
37. Gould K, Lewis T (2017) Green gentrification: Urban sustainability and the struggle for environmental justice. Routledge
38. Lyytimäki J, Petersen LK, Normander B, Bezák P (2008) Nature as a nuisance? Ecosystem services and disservices to urban lifestyle. Environ Sci (Ruse) 5:161–172. https://doi.org/10.1080/15693430802055524
39. Moffat AJ (2016) Communicating the benefits of urban trees: a critical review. Arboric J 38:64–82. https://doi.org/10.1080/03071375.2016.1163111
40. Martek I, Edwards DJ, Seaton S, Jones D (2022) An appraisal of Australia's approach to promoting urban sustainability. Built Environ Proj Asset Manag 12:262–276. https://doi.org/10.1108/BEPAM-07-2020-0130
41. United Nations (2015) Paris Agreement. Paris, France
42. Commonwealth of Australia (2024) International climate action. In: https://www.dcceew.gov.au/climate-change/international-climate-action
43. United Nations Environment Program (1992) Convention on Biological Diversity. United Nations Environment Program, Rio de Janeiro
44. United Nations Environment Program (2022) Kunming-Montreal global biodiversity framework. In: Convention on Biological Diversity. Montreal, Canada
45. Department of Climate Change, Energy, Environment and Water (2024) Australia's Strategy for Nature 2024–2030. Canberra
46. United Nations (1992) Report of the United Nations Conference on Environment and Development. In: Rio de Janeiro. United Nations, New York, Rio de Janeiro
47. UNECE Forestry, Housing and Land Management (2024) Urban trees for climate and SDGs: mobilizing action at the local, national and international level. In:

UNECE.org. https://w3.unece.org/sdg2024/story-11.html#:~:text=Trees%20and%20forests%20in%20and,15%20(life%20on%20land). Accessed 27 Sep 2024
48. Salbitano F, Borelli S, Conigliaro M, Chen Y (2016) Guidelines on urban and peri-urban forestry. Rome
49. United Nations (2016) The new urban agenda. Quito, Ecuador
50. Pokharel S, Archer F (2020) Habitat-III and the new urban agenda: implications for Australia. Aust J Emerg Manag 66–72
51. Commonwealth of Australia (2024) A National Urban Policy for Australia. https://www.infrastructure.gov.au/have-your-say/national-urban-policy-australia
52. Commonwealth of Australia (2024) National Urban Policy consultation draft
53. World Health Organisation (2023) Assessing the value of urban green and blue spaces for health and well-being. Copenhagen
54. CSIRO Urban Monitor. In: CSIRO Australia. https://www.csiro.au/en/research/technology-space/data/urban-monitor. Accessed 15 Jun 2023
55. Western Australian Planning Commission (2018) Better urban forest planning: A guide to support the enhancement of urban forests in Western Australia
56. Konijnendijk van den Bosch C (2021) Promoting health and wellbeing through urban forests—introducing the 3-30-300 rule. In: LinkedIn. https://iucnurbanalliance.org/promoting-health-and-wellbeing-through-urban-forests-introducing-the-3-30-300-rule/. Accessed 27 Jul 2023
57. Parker J, Simpson GD (2020) A case study balancing predetermined targets and real-world constraints to guide optimum urban tree canopy cover for Perth, Western Australia. Forests 11:1–19. https://doi.org/10.3390/f11111128
58. Jacobs B, Mikhailovich N, Delaney C (2014) Benchmarking Australia's urban tree canopy: An i-tree assessment
59. Greener Spaces Better Places (2014) Where are all the trees? An analysis of tree canopy cover in urban Australia
60. Hurley J, Amati M, Deilami K, et al (2020) Where will all the trees be?—an assessment of urban forest cover and management for Australian cities. Prepared for Hort Innovation by the Centre for Urban Research, RMIT University, Melbourne
61. Amati M, Boruff B, Caccetta P, et al (2017) Where should all the trees go? Investigating the impact of tree canopy cover on socio-economic status and wellbeing in LGAs. Prepared for Hort Innovation by the Centre for Urban Research, RMIT University, Melbourne, Australia
62. ABS (2002) Year Book Australia, 1.0130. Land Tenure
63. ABS (2022) Land and housing supply indicators. In: Australian Bureau of Statistics. https://www.abs.gov.au/statistics/industry/building-and-construction/land-and-housing-supply-indicators/latest-release#key-statistics. Accessed 15 Jun 2023
64. R & R Fazzolari Pty Ltd v Parramatta City Council (2009) 237 CLR 603
65. Lee SJ, Longcore T, Rich C, Wilson JP (2017) Increased home size and hardscape decreases urban forest cover in Los Angeles County's single-family residential neighborhoods. Urban For Urban Green 24:222–235. https://doi.org/10.1016/j.ufug.2017.03.004
66. Morgenroth J, O'Neil-Dunne J, Apiolaza LA (2017) Redevelopment and the urban forest: A study of tree removal and retention during demolition activities. Appl Geogr 82:1–10. https://doi.org/10.1016/j.apgeog.2017.02.011
67. Ordóñez-Barona C, Bush J, Hurley J et al (2021) International approaches to protecting and retaining trees on private urban land. J Environ Manage 285:112081. https://doi.org/10.1016/j.jenvman.2021.112081
68. Saunders A, Duncan J, Hurley J et al (2020) Leaf my neighbourhood alone! Predicting the influence of densification on residential tree canopy cover in Perth. Landsc Urban Plan 199:103804. https://doi.org/10.1016/j.landurbplan.2020.103804
69. Torquato PR, Szota C, Hahs AK et al (2025) Insufficient space: Prioritizing large tree species and planting designs still fail to meet urban forest canopy targets. Landsc Urban Plan 256:105287. https://doi.org/10.1016/j.landurbplan.2024.105287
70. Marcos Martinez R, Soonsawad N, Dias Baptista M et al (2025) Challenges and strategies in meeting urban tree canopy targets: A scenario discovery analysis to guide urban forest planning

in new developments. Trees, Forests and People 19:100787. https://doi.org/10.1016/j.tfp.2025.100787
71. Brunner J, Cozens P (2013) "Where have all the trees gone?" Urban consolidation and the demise of urban vegetation: A case study from Western Australia. Plan Pract Res 28:231–255. https://doi.org/10.1080/02697459.2012.733525

Chapter 2
Individual Tree Protection

Abstract Tree loss on private land has been identified as one of the primary drivers behind urban canopy decline in Australia. The primary mechanism for slowing this loss is to require approval to be obtained for the removal of specified trees. This may be achieved by a registration process or by the operation of an automatic protection. With registration, a tree may be identified as having particular cultural or other value and is then listed on a register (often called a Significant Tree Register) from which time it is protected. Automatic protections apply where a tree meets specified physical measurement criteria such that it receives protection without the need to be registered (known as 'blanket' protection). In many local and state jurisdictions, both mechanisms are used simultaneously. Local or state legislation sets out the criteria a tree must meet in order to be protected and the circumstances in which tree removal can be permitted or a proposed development refused. Local government is normally the administering body and makes the initial decision on any tree removal application. Disputes between local government and landowners or developers are common, and often relate to the reasons for a refusal to permit a tree to be removed.

2.1 Introduction

Recent research has identified tree loss on private land as a key factor behind urban canopy decline trends in Australia [1–3]. The regulatory controls applicable to the protection of trees on private land have accordingly become a focus of interest across a range of stakeholders, including researchers, urban forest interest groups and government bodies.

In Australia, the main regulatory control for preventing tree loss on private land is to require the landowner to obtain approval for the removal of a tree, with associated penalties for failure to obtain approval. This type of approval requirement mechanism is very common, as approvals are ordinarily required for many activities on private land, such as building new structures. In this way, the approving body (normally local government) can require trees on private land to be retained and can stipulate conditions as needed to safeguard the future life of the tree.

E. J. Scaife, *Urban Tree Protection on Private Land*,
SpringerBriefs in Law, https://doi.org/10.1007/978-981-95-1857-9_2

There are essentially two ways to engage this type of control in Australia:

- Protection by registration. A tree may be identified as having particular cultural or other specified value and is then listed on a register (often called a Significant Tree Register) from which time it is protected.[1]
- Blanket protection for all trees meeting set criteria. Any tree meeting specified criteria (usually minimum physical measurement criteria) receives automatic protection without the need to be listed.

Many local jurisdictions in Australia have both mechanisms available for use. However, in the Northern Territory neither mechanism is used. In South Australia, although some trees are labelled 'significant' under state law, this only relates to blanket protections for very large trees and not to a registration process.

There is another regulatory mechanism to protect trees on private lands through heritage protection laws. All states and territories have laws that provide for heritage protections, and there are additional protections in Australia's federal cultural heritage laws.[2] These normally operate by way of listing on a heritage register. Heritage places or features within a heritage area can include trees [4] and, in this way, heritage laws operate to protect some trees on private land.[3] Apart from the Northern Territory, where neither of the above tree protection mechanisms apply, tree registers operate as a type of heritage protection specifically relating to trees, with additional scope for application beyond heritage values, as discussed below.

2.2 Tree Registers

2.2.1 Establishing a Tree Register

Many local governments in Australia have created tree registers. These are often known as 'Significant Tree Registers' or 'Exceptional Tree Registers'. Trees within the relevant jurisdiction identified as being significant, and that are not excluded from registration, may be listed on the register. Once registered (or, in some jurisdictions, once nominated), legal protections apply that are intended to prevent the registered tree being damaged or removed without council[4] approval.

The registration process varies between jurisdictions. Listings are generally created following nomination by a member of the public. Some registers require

[1] Some jurisdictions also provide for interim protections to apply from the time a tree is nominated until the time a decision is made on registering the tree.

[2] For a list of all Australian federal heritage laws, see https://whc.unesco.org/en/statesparties/au/Laws.

[3] See, for example, https://www.heritage.vic.gov.au/heritage-listings/state-heritage-listing.

[4] For simplification of language, the word 'council' is used in this Chapter to include state, territory and local governments, unless context demands otherwise.

an arboriculture report to be prepared to support the listing of the tree[5] and, where the tree is on private land, most either require the consent of the relevant landowner or provide an opportunity for the landowner to make a submission in the course of listing. Usually, a single tree is listed but most registers also allow for groups of trees to be listed as one entry. Most allow for trees of any origin (native or exotic) or age[6] to be listed.

Some councils specify preconditions to registration. For example, some registers set out minimum tree size criteria. There are examples of registers that do not allow trees on private land to be listed on the register—in such cases this mechanism is rendered ineffective for protection of trees on private land.[7] However, most registers apply to both public and private land.

Ultimately, the decision to list a tree on a register is a discretionary decision made by the council. In the context of a dispute between neighbours, the NSW Court of Appeal considered whether a council had a duty to list a tree on its register if it could be demonstrated that the tree met the required criteria, commenting[8] that there was no such duty and, in any event, the landowner would have had a right to be heard on the listing prior to it being made [5].

2.2.2 Trees Eligible for Registration

The meaning of significant (or exceptional) differs between jurisdictions: some registers set out an extensive range of values that are included in the definition of 'significant', whereas others have a limited definition extending only to a few key values. An approach taken by some local governments is to mirror the provisions set out in the National Trusts' Register of Significant Trees (*National Trusts' Tree Register*). The National Trusts' Tree Register is non-statutory and therefore offers no legal protections, but some local governments have used it as a guide to the creation of a formal tree register.

By way of illustration, The National Trusts' Tree Register provides that a tree needs to meet any one of the following criteria to be considered significant:

Horticultural

- Horticultural or genetic value
- Important source of seed or propagating stock
- Particularly resistant to disease or exposure

---

[5] These can be expensive and may act as a deterrent to nomination.

[6] In Melbourne, a two-year-old tree was listed as part of a formal ceremony.

[7] For example, the Shire of Serpentine Jarrahdale in WA created a Significant Tree Register that does not include nominated trees on private property or on land controlled by government agencies, noting that these may be included at a later stage: see https://www.sjshire.wa.gov.au/community/health-and-environment/trees/significant-tree-register.aspx.

[8] In *obiter dicta*, as the decision did not turn on this issue.

- Species or variety that is rare or of a very localised distribution
- Particularly old or venerable
- Remnant native vegetation
- Outstanding for its height, trunk circumference or canopy spread
- An outstanding example of the species

Social

- Unique location or context
- Contribution to landscape
- Associated with Aboriginal activities
- Important landmark
- Spiritual and religious associations
- Contemporary association with the community

Historic

- Forms part of an historic park, garden or town
- Commemorates an occasion e.g. memorial or ceremonial plantings such as Avenue of Honour
- Associated with an important event
- Associated with an important person, group or institution

Aesthetic

- A really great looking tree
- Exhibits curious growth form or unusual physical features whether naturally occurring, resulting from natural events or human intervention
- Is a better than an average example of its species, or in its particular location [6, p 3]

Beyond these commonly used criteria, many councils have opted to extend the values to ecological significance, to include (for example) trees that contribute to the integrity of an ecological community, or are a significant habitat element for a threatened species.[9]

Some councils record detailed information on the way in which the tree is valued. This material can be quite interesting and has even inspired poetry [7].

2.2.3 Exclusions

Once a tree is nominated or identified for its significance, the next step in the assessment process involves the council considering whether the tree is excluded from protection. The precise reasons for exclusion vary between jurisdictions, but reasons commonly specified by councils are set out below.

---

[9] For example, City of Mandurah (WA), see: https://www.mandurah.wa.gov.au/-/media/files/com/downloads/live/trees-and-verges/significant-tree-register/signifcant-tree-register-brochure.pdf.

2.2.3.1 Weedy Species

Most councils have lists of specific tree species that will not be protected.

2.2.3.2 Safety Risk or Hazardous

Some trees are identified as a safety risk to people, or hazardous to assets such as buildings or vehicles. This is often due to a combination of the tree's location (have regard to human activity nearby) and its propensity to drop limbs or likelihood of falling.[10] In cases involving consideration of this issue in the context of tree removal applications, there is often a question of degree in deciding whether these issues simply relate to ordinary maintenance.[11] To assist with determining this issue, the NSW Land and Environment Court developed a tree dispute principle:

> For people who live in urban environments, it is appropriate to expect that some degree of house exterior and grounds maintenance will be required in order to appreciate and retain the aesthetic and environmental benefits of having trees in such an urban environment. In particular, it is reasonable to expect people living in such an environment might need to clean the gutters and the surrounds of their houses on a regular basis.
>
> The dropping of leaves, flowers, fruit, seeds or small elements of deadwood by urban trees ordinarily will not provide the basis for ordering removal of or intervention with an urban tree [8, para 20]

2.2.3.3 Short Future Life Expectancy

In *Lacey v City of Burnside* [9], a future life expectancy of ten years was confirmed to be sufficient to support retention of a protected tree. The necessity of this factor is questionable, particularly where applicable ecological values such as provision of nesting habitat would continue beyond the tree's life expectancy (see under 'Dead' below).

2.2.3.4 Diseased

Diseased trees may be considered poor candidates for protection, particularly where the disease may spread to other trees or render the tree hazardous. Termites are generally not considered to be a disease [10].

---

[10] In the ACT this has been held to include an assessment of future risk [10].

[11] See, for example, the discussion of values and risks in *Sheehan v Santosa* [47].

2.2.3.5 Dead

In some jurisdictions, dead trees are excluded from being registered. However, there is authority supporting the view that a once-living registered tree, despite having died, may retain its registered status where the values it is providing still apply, such as visual amenity or nesting habitat [11]. Some jurisdictions now refer to this criterion as conditional upon there being no remaining value associated with the dead tree. Under new laws in the ACT, registered trees that die naturally may be removed from the register [12, Div 4.5] however, any unregistered dead native tree over a certain size is automatically protected due to its presumed habitat value [12, Div 4.5, Cl 11(1)(b)].

2.2.3.6 Too Close to Existing Built Structures

Some councils specify precise distances for determining whether a tree is too close to built structures. This varies between jurisdictions, with approximate ranges from 2 m to 10 m. When this criterion operates as an exemption to blanket protections (discussed in the following section), any allowance for proximity to built structures (even 2 m) can negatively impact overall canopy cover in an urban area. For example, Sydney's Inner West Council introduced a proximity exemption of 2 m, leading to an immediate increase in approved tree removal applications:

> In a briefing to councillors last month, staff said they had approved applications to cut down 915 trees after the policy giving landholders the right to remove trees within two metres of homes came into effect last February.
>
> This was more than double the 373 trees removed in 2019 and about 409 trees cleared in 2018.
>
> It meant tree canopy in the inner west fell from 17.77 per cent to 17.36 per cent - below the city-wide average of 23 per cent. [13]

These exclusions are similar (sometimes identical) to exemptions from blanket protections, which are noted in the following section of this chapter.

2.2.4 *Enforcement*

Registration creates a legal requirement, usually under planning law provisions, that the landowner must obtain council approval prior to carrying out any tree-damaging activity. Failure to obtain approval is an offence for which penalties apply. This legal requirement continues to apply regardless of a subsequent sale of the land. Although a registered tree would not normally be recorded on the land title, it may be noted in the sale documents when property ownership is transferred.[12]

---

[12] See, for example, *Krajinovic v Heath* [17].

Enforcement of significant tree protections is, within the bounds of the legal provisions, often a matter for local government policy. If permission to remove a registered tree is refused, a landowner may appeal to the relevant court or tribunal where the council's decision will be reviewed. Where a development is proceeding and a significant tree is to be retained, the development approval will normally include conditions for protecting the tree during and after development.[13]

Where a registered tree is removed or damaged without approval, the council can take action to stop the damage from starting or continuing. See, for example, *Sunline Developments Pty Ltd v City of Campbelltown and Genesis Equity* [14], where several steps were taken by the council to prevent tree damage from continuing, including seeking an injunction. Where it is too late to prevent the damage or removal, the council can take steps to impose a penalty on the offender. Across Australia, the range of penalties varies widely, from $500[14] to $1.1 million.[15] The two most significant factors determining the maximum penalty applicable are the state or territory jurisdiction in which the offence occurred, and whether the council chooses to issue an infringement notice or prosecute the offence in court. For example, in WA an infringement notice fine is $500 whereas the maximum penalty for a prosecuted offence is $200,000 plus $25,000 per day for a continuing offence [15, s223].

The deterrent effect of penalties is important. In support of setting high penalties in new urban forest legislation in the ACT, the explanatory statement referred to the need to create a deterrent effect, particularly where a person is considering developing a property for financial gain [16]. The courts have taken a similar view. The Supreme Court of Tasmania considered the penalties imposed by a magistrate where the applicant had lopped two significant trees and demolished an asbestos building without approvals, noting:

> ...[I]n my view, the learned magistrate was correct to conclude that general deterrence was the predominant aspect of punishment. That is, the principal purpose of sentence was to deter others from acting in disregard of the planning laws, thus placing personal interest ahead of public interest. That is particularly so when, as here, the offending development work involves a commercial aspect. There is a strong need to ensure compliance with planning laws in respect of such developments [17, para 30]

The Court found it was not manifestly excessive to impose fines totalling $225,000 (for multiple offences, including tree damage) amounting to approximately 62% of the maximum possible amount.

Some councils report difficulties obtaining evidence to support a court prosecution, leaving minor infringement notices as the only practical option for enforcement. They are concerned that this creates little deterrence for would-be offenders, who can often simply absorb the anticipated infringement fine amount into their project's planned cost-base. This has prompted some councils to seek state law reform to increase penalties to an appropriate level to act as a deterrent [18]. The same evidentiary problem has been addressed in other jurisdictions by making the offence one

---

[13] See Chap. 6 for a discussion of the Australian Standard on tree protection during construction.

[14] For an offence in WA where the council issues an infringement notice.

[15] For an offence in NSW prosecuted in the NSW Land and Environment Court.

of strict liability (to remove the burden of proving knowledge on the part of the landowner), or by allowing search and seizure powers so an enforcing authority may enter private property to stop offences and/or obtain evidence for a prosecution [12].

2.2.5 *Effectiveness of Tree Registers*

It appears that relatively few trees are listed on significant tree registers in Australia. Although no studies have focussed on numbers of listings, some studies have touched on this topic, indicating that many registers contain fewer than 200 listings [19–22]. Of these, even fewer listings are for trees growing on private land. For example, the City of Ballarat has over 4000 trees listed on its Exceptional Tree Register, but only 91 of these are on private land [23]. Clark et al. [3] speculated that the low numbers may be caused by difficulties in the process of registration, such as a passive recruitment method relying on public nominations. For example, the City of Moonee Valley changed its tree registration process from public nominations only to a proactive update process including recommendations by external consultants [3]. Following the first update, the register more than doubled in size (including trees on private land) [24]. Another possibility is that the criteria for registration are often limited and strictly applied, such that few trees are able to qualify for registration at all. Whatever the cause (or causes) may be, the low numbers of trees listed on registers reduces the effectiveness of this mechanism as a way of reversing urban canopy loss [3].

There is evidence of landowner respect for registered trees. In a study carried out in New Zealand, where similar significant tree registers operate, a localised spate of redevelopment activity following an earthquake was monitored for landowners' tree removal behaviour during demolition. The results showed, amongst other things, that all trees protected by listing on a significant tree register were retained in place throughout the demolition, prompting the authors to comment that 'their status as significant trees may have played a role in their retention' [20]. [p 8] The National Trusts of Australia, that together operate an informal Australia-wide significant tree register, state that 'most owners take pride in the fact that that they own a classified tree, and take responsibility for its proper management' [6, p 3] This may be due to landowner involvement in the listing decision.

In Auckland, New Zealand, blanket tree protections (discussed below) were removed by a suite of legislative changes known as 'Auckland Isthmus', leaving only a tree register in place (the Schedule of Notable Trees (SoNT)). A study was conducted to determine the parameters of the consequent reduced protection of trees on private land, in the context of biodiversity support. This study identified not only the low numbers of trees, but also the dominance of certain species on Auckland's tree register as causing problems for safeguarding biodiversity:

> Within the Auckland Isthmus, tree protection on private land has been reduced to just 15% of what was previously protected through blanket tree protection policies, as the SoNT remains the only source of tree protection in these areas. This schedule is dominated by large numbers

> of a few popular tree species, which strongly reflect Auckland's cultural heritage. Our study suggests that the case-by-case protection of individual trees provides insufficient protection to safeguard urban biodiversity [25, p 120]

By contrast, in the USA, where similar issues arise, a study conducted in Florida showed a correlation between cities with heritage or significant tree protections and greater urban canopy cover (a 6.7% increase). The explanation posited was that heritage/significant trees tended to be older and therefore larger, providing greater canopy cover per tree than other trees [26]. However, it was unclear what was covered by 'heritage/significant tree protections' in the survey conducted and whether these protections included trees on private land. It is therefore difficult to draw any useful conclusions about how the results of this study might translate to the effectiveness of tree registers on private land in Australia.

2.3 Blanket Protections

2.3.1 Criteria for Protection

Blanket protection of trees is created by specifying criteria that, if met by an individual tree, means that approval is required for the removal of, or damage to, the tree. The predominant threshold method is based on specified tree dimension criteria. However, other methods are also used, often in addition (and as alternatives) to dimensional criteria, including location, specific nominated species, or having particular environmental value [27]. Location and environmental value bases are discussed in the following chapter on protecting forested areas.

The dimension criteria are generally tree height, trunk circumference and canopy diameter. Where all three are used, they are usually set as alternatives to each other, so a tree only needs to meet one of the criteria to be protected, rather than being required to meet all three.

The measurements used vary widely between jurisdictions. In South Australia two recent studies were carried out to compare the measurement criteria across a number of jurisdictions, to determine whether the measurements used in South Australia were aligned with those used in other similar locations in Australia. The first study was carried out by the Conservation Council of South Australia in 2021. This assessed 48 jurisdictions (including SA) for tree measurement criteria used in blanket protections [28]. The second study was carried out by the University of Adelaide for the South Australian Attorney General in 2022. This study was designed to assess and expand upon the first study and to make a series of recommendations for improving Adelaide's tree protection laws. The second study assessed 101 jurisdictions for tree measurement criteria [27]. Both studies focussed on jurisdictions with similar characteristics to Adelaide, in terms of rainfall, urbanisation and population density.

Both studies reported a wide range of measurements for blanket tree protections in Australia, and both concluded that South Australia's protections were limited by

Table 2.1 Range of tree measurement threshold criteria for blanket protections in Australia

Criterion/Range	Lowest	Highest	Average
Tree height	2 m [28]	12 m [27]	6.32 m [27]
Trunk circumference	7.5 cm [28]	200 cm [28]	53 cm [27]
Canopy diameter	2 m [28]	5 m [28]	3.5 m [27]

applying only one criterion and by the measurement threshold being positioned at the high end of the range for that criterion [27, 28]. The range of measurements reported in these studies is set out in Table 2.1. Although based on a subset of jurisdictions, these ranges illustrate the variability in blanket protections across Australia.

2.3.1.1 Tree Height

According to Belder et al. [27], tree height is the most common criterion used in blanket protections. It is useful because it can be easy to gauge from eyesight at ground level by reference to other common structures. However, problems have been identified. When the height requirement is high (above 6 m) it can become more difficult to accurately assess without specialist measuring devices. Tree height is also able to be reduced by allowable pruning.

2.3.1.2 Trunk Circumference / Diameter

Trunk circumference is also a very commonly used criterion in blanket protections. Trunk circumference can be measured from the ground with a standard measuring tape. There are various heights specified for taking the measurement, with ground level, above ground level, 1 m and 1.4 m all commonly used. The resultant calculation of diameter at breast height (*dbh*) is also used in some jurisdictions (a calculation based on a circumference measurement taken at 1.4 m above ground level). *Dbh* has been shown to positively correlate with a tree's height and canopy diameter, allowing those criteria to be estimated from *dbh* [29]. It is also difficult to impact *dbh* by pruning or any other method. Some problems arise where trees have multiple trunks. For this reason, most jurisdictions specifying trunk circumference also allow for alternative combined trunk measurements where multiple trunks occur. Despite the ease of measuring trunk circumference, disputes over trunk measurements have occurred, for example where the tree has developed bulges in the trunk [30], or where the natural ground level is sloped so the correct point at which to measure circumference is unclear [14].

2.3.1.3 Canopy Diameter

Canopy diameter (or 'crown spread') is the least common criterion used in blanket protections. It is useful for councils because canopy cover is the metric used for canopy targets and is easy to measure using satellite imagery without requiring access to the property. However, it is difficult for a landowner to assess accurately from the ground. Canopy diameter can also be altered by allowable pruning.

2.3.2 Problems with Measurement Criteria

One problem with dimension criteria is that precision in measurement is difficult to achieve, even with specialist measuring devices. This leads to differing measurement results of the same tree: for example, in a dispute involving an assessment of tree measurements, the Court prepared a table to show the differing measurement evidence from two expert arborists (Table 2.2).

In that case, on either view, the dimensions were above the required criteria, but disputes can and do occur in cases where the parties' measurements fall on opposite sides of the required criteria.

Another issue with tree dimension measurements is the ability of a landowner to accurately measure a tree without specialist skills or devices. At present, only trunk circumference and low height measurements are reliably accurate using simple measuring devices. However, recent developments in smartphone applications may allow urban tree dimensions to be measured using a combination of data including satellite imagery and photographs. A study designed to test smartphone applications for urban tree measurement found that '*the use of smartphones for tree measurement is a practical and reliable option because it allows the accurate assessment of several tree parameters with a single device*' [32, p 120]. The use of smartphone applications may solve some of the problems associated with tree measurements in the future.

There are also particular policy issues with the use of higher tree dimensions as threshold criteria, because this approach does not capture smaller trees that might be desirable to protect. The lower the threshold, the more trees will be covered and therefore more canopy cover protected. There are other impacts to consider as well. For example, in a drying climate, trees may not reach previously expected dimensions, so over time a fixed high threshold is likely to protect a dwindling number of trees. Furthermore, high thresholds can lead to favouring protection of larger species over smaller ones.[16] There is a recently identified trend for private landowners to plant small and medium sized tree species in gardens, rather than large species [33], again leading to protection of fewer trees over time. Finally, fixed

[16] Some jurisdictions address this issue by specifying lower criteria for certain smaller or slower-growing species. However, this creates additional complexity for landowners and councils in determining whether a tree is protected.

Table 2.2 Showing two expert arborists' assessments of the same tree (extract from Jarvis Property No 3 Pty Ltd v City of Holdfast Bay Assessment Panel [31] [at 33])

Arborist	Species	Circumference (metres)	Height (metres)	Spread (metres)				Age (years)	Life expectancy (years)
				N	S	E	W		
Dr Nicolle	Eucalyptus camaldulensis	4.2	22	12.0	11.5	11	7.5	80–150 (mature)	20+
Mr Cassar	Eucalyptus camaldulensis	4.3	23.4	10.8	12	9.2	5.8	90+ (mature)	20+

high criteria do not allow the flexibility to protect younger trees that may be needed to improve the overall resilience of the urban forest into the future.

Putting lower threshold dimensions in place may solve some of these problems and is seen as a way to increase the number of trees protected. In 2023, the ACT introduced new legislation to create stronger protections for urban trees, which included reducing the previous threshold dimensions from height 12 m to 8 m, canopy width 12 m to 8 m and trunk circumference 1.5 m to 1 m [12, 34]. In South Australia, a 2023 Parliamentary Inquiry Interim Report recommended that the threshold trunk size dimensions for regulated trees in South Australia should be reduced from 2 m to 1 m, and that canopy spread should be introduced as an additional alternative threshold criterion [35].

2.3.3 *Removing the Threshold Criteria*

In recent times, some jurisdictions have taken the approach of bypassing measurement threshold criteria altogether. These jurisdictions specify that 'all trees' within the local government area are protected and then allow an exemption for trees under a certain height (normally quite low, usually 3–5 m) or a small trunk circumference. Although measurements are still used in relation to exemption criteria, this is simplified where the exemption is trunk circumference or where the height measurement is low enough to measure accurately from the ground.

In cases of unlawful tree removal, the use of an exemption rather than a threshold criterion will ordinarily place the onus on the landowner to prove a tree is exempt (including on the basis of height measurements), rather than the initial onus being on the council to prove the tree is protected. This difference may help to remove barriers to enforcement and support the deterrent effect of penalties.

2.3.4 *Exemptions*

There is a (potentially significant) difference between an exclusion and an exemption. An exclusion operates at the outset to exclude a tree from obtaining protected status at all. However, an exemption works *after* the protections apply, to allow the protection to specifically be removed from certain trees. The same substantive reason, for example, a diseased tree, would therefore be likely to exclude a tree from a Significant Tree Register because this exclusion would normally be applied as part of the decision to list a tree. However, the same diseased tree might be covered by blanket protections but could be exempt under a specific exemption for diseased trees. The difference may seem irrelevant but there is an important operational effect of exemptions: a landowner is usually required to apply for an exemption. In cases where a tree covered by blanket protections is removed without permission, an offence is therefore committed even where an exemption might have applied.

This means it is important to understand the operational effect of exclusions and exemptions applying to blanket tree protections. Usually there are both exclusions and exemptions. This will depend on the precise wording of the legislation in each jurisdiction. For the sake of simplicity, in the following paragraphs 'exemption' is used for both types (unless otherwise specified).

Exemptions apply in all jurisdictions that have blanket protections. The more common exemptions tend to relate to the same reasons as for tree registers, discussed above in detail:

- Weedy species
- Safety risk or hazardous
- Short future life expectancy
- Diseased
- Dead
- Too close to existing built structures
- Required by other regulations, such as fire protection measures.

Other matters that are sometimes included as exemptions, but in some jurisdictions are not included or are specifically excluded as reasons for exemption:

- Allergic reaction caused by the tree
- Blocking views
- Blocking light (including light to solar panels)
- In the case of a proposed development, that alternative solutions have been considered (tree protections and development are discussed below).

2.3.5 Tree Damaging Activity

Generally, where a tree is protected, approval is required for any activity that may damage the tree. This is normally a defined term in legislation and usually includes any activity that could harm or kill a tree (such as removal, poisoning or damage to roots). 'Hard' pruning is usually included as a tree damaging activity, with an associated definition of allowable pruning that often sets a percentage allowance[17] and requires compliance with the Australian Standard on Pruning Amenity Trees.[18]

Many disputes over tree removal applications turn on the question of whether pruning will be sufficient to address concerns over safety and potential damage to structures, or whether the tree needs to be removed.[19] This type of legal dispute often involves an assessment of risk, applied in the context of the relevant legislative

---

[17] The way the allowance is framed can be important: in *Corporation of the City of Unley v Crichton (No 2)* [48] the pruning percentage allowance would be calculated differently depending on whether the crown of the tree was defined to include dead limbs and diseased leaves.

[18] See Chap. 7 for a discussion of the Australian Standard on Pruning Amenity Trees.

[19] See, for example, *Ditara Pty Ltd v Corporation of the City of Norwood Payneham & St Peters Assessment Manager* [36] and *Lacey v City of Burnside* [9].

wording. A standardised tree risk assessment process developed by the International Society of Arborists known as 'TRAQ'[20] is sometimes used by arborists to make this type of assessment, although the TRAQ method does not always find favour with courts [31, 36]. In the ACT, the Supreme Court considered that the risk to potential future occupiers of the land was a relevant consideration in this assessment [10].

By way of illustration of the overall decision process in 'pruning' disputes, the following extract sets out the findings of the court in a recent South Australian case:

We find:

- the tree is a significant tree that warrants protection as that it makes an important contribution to the character and amenity of the local area and forms a notable visual element to the landscape of the local area;
- the tree poses an unacceptable risk to public and private safety due to limb drop;
- pruning is a reasonable remedial treatment, and the appellant has not demonstrated that would be ineffective; and
- the tree does not warrant removal in the first instance [36, at 56]

The wording of 'significant tree' in South Australian state tree legislation is not associated with a tree register; it refers instead to a subset of larger dimension regulated trees.

2.3.6 *Enforcement*

In Australia, it is possible that enforcement behaviour is relevant to the impact of tree protections, but there is little research examining this question. Clark et al. found that difficulty with enforcement was a relatively consistent factor raised by local government professionals as a cause of canopy loss [3]. Enforcement behaviour patterns may be reflected in the number or percentage of tree removal approvals granted each year. In the research conducted by Clark et al. it was noted that one jurisdiction provided data that revealed a permit approval rate of 72% on private land over a six-year period [3]. If similar rates apply in other jurisdictions, it might be expected that blanket tree protections could have only a minor impact on canopy cover decline on private land, even where the protections in place would otherwise be considered strong.

The fees and costs associated with tree removal applications may also be relevant as a disincentive. Where permits are required, there are often application fees payable. These tend to be relatively low (under $500) across most jurisdictions [27]. Some jurisdictions also require an arborist's report to be supplied in support of the removal application [27]. The cost of an arborist's report reportedly ranges from $450–$2000 [37].

---

[20] Tree Risk Assessment Qualification (see https://www.isa-arbor.com/Credentials/ISA-Tree-Risk-Assessment-Qualification).

The other aspect of enforcement relates to the imposition of penalties following unlawful tree damage. This is discussed above in relation to tree registers: the same factors apply to blanket protections. Enforcement behaviour in relation to tree damage offences may be reflected, in part, by the number of cases disputed in the relevant courts or tribunals. Apart from the present review (which is limited) there appears to be no other review of these cases to date.

2.3.7 Effectiveness of Blanket Protections

Blanket tree protections in Australia are increasingly being engaged to support a wide range of important policy aims in the urban environment. These aims include canopy increase, urban heat island mitigation, biodiversity support, support for freshwater processes and social equity. Many local governments have devised urban forest strategies setting out these policy aims. The question arises as to whether the existing blanket protection mechanisms are capable of supporting these policy goals on private land. In other words, are blanket tree protections effective?

There is little research in Australia examining the impact of blanket tree protections on canopy cover or other policy aims. The Greener Spaces Better Places series of research reports suggested that the overall trend of canopy decline was evidence of tree protection mechanisms failing to support canopy increase on private land. Further, the failure was sufficient to counter any gains made on public land, meaning that most LGAs recorded canopy decline regardless of the type of tree protections available, or whether there was an urban forest strategy in place and how successful the strategy was on public land [1, 38, 39]. Clark et al. conducted research into the perspectives of local government professionals on the efficacy of tree protections, to explore potential reasons for canopy decline on private land. This produced useful information on the reasons, but did not attempt to link those reasons to quantifiable urban forest metrics such as rate of canopy decline [3].

In the USA, a number of studies have been conducted to better understand the effect of similar tree protections. Some of these studies have found that blanket tree protections are correlated to positive impacts on urban forest metrics such as tree height and canopy cover, and to related policy aims such as urban heat island mitigation. Other USA studies have indicated that the mere existence of tree protection controls is not a good predictor of canopy cover, suggesting instead that the enforcement behaviour of the relevant governing body may be a better predictor [40].

2.4 Tree Protections and Development

2.4.1 *Impacts of Development on Canopy Cover*

With canopy decline on private land becoming a focus of interest, studies involving interviews with local government planning officers indicated that development activity was a primary driver of mature tree loss on private land [1, 3]. These findings were partially supported by a quantitative study of tree loss and major development activity in the City of Melbourne, spanning 2008–2016 (*City of Melbourne study*) [41]. The findings showed that, although much tree cover was both lost and gained over time, there was a net loss of trees on private land and a large proportion of that net loss occurred at sites of major development activity. In addition, development activity on private land was a proximate cause of *public* tree loss in the immediate vicinity of the development. In other words, development activity negatively impacts urban tree canopy, not only on private land but also on adjacent public land.[21] In the context of net canopy loss on private land, the authors concluded:

> Clearly, major private developments were the key driver of tree canopy cover loss in private lands during these nine years [41, p 9]

This problem is not limited to major development activity, nor to Australia. In New Zealand, Morgenroth et al. [20], investigated whether trees were retained or removed during the demolition stage of redevelopment. The research team found an opportunity for data collection resulting from a wide-scale urban residential redevelopment pattern following a series of earthquakes. The study showed that trees with a small crown area were disproportionately removed during demolition, in particular those located within 0.7 m of the building to be demolished. The study also found that the proportion of tree removals increased with increasing land value, the authors noting: '…this result implies that the possibility of economic gains from redevelopment of high value land may provide incentive for tree removal' [20, p 8]. In total, building demolition resulted in a canopy reduction of 19.7% of the original canopy cover on the properties surveyed.

In Poland, a study was conducted of urban tree canopy over a ten-year period mapping canopy loss correlations with land use. In that time period there was a six-month window where blanket protections were almost entirely removed, leaving landowners to 'vote with their chainsaws'. The study showed a substantial increase in tree removals over that window, particularly on land classed as 'unclassified and unmanaged green space', which equated to vacant lots. The authors speculated that these land parcels were seen as likely to be redeveloped in the future, with owners taking the opportunity to prepare their land for future sale, commenting:

[21] The authors of the study speculated that this was related to the construction phase and large vehicle access either necessitating removal or causing fatal damage to tree roots of trees on surrounding public land. Ibid, p9.

> ...[L]andowners often believe that their plot would be easier to sell without trees, especially when it comes to undeveloped plots. Indeed, most building investments in Poland start with removing all existing vegetation, trees in particular [42, p 8][22]

In Western Australia, where the introduction of blanket protections is relatively recent, there is evidence supporting a similar tendency for landowners to remove trees as part of the development process. For example, the City of Nedlands reported 'a 58% decline in canopy cover on the 244 private lots which have undergone significant development or subdivision from 2009 to 2016' [43].

2.4.2 Conflicts Between Tree Protection and Development

Where blanket protections exist, there is often specific legislative provision dealing with the interaction between development and tree retention. Some jurisdictions allow exemptions for development using the concept of reasonableness, such as a development plan then applicable in Gawler, South Australia, which provided that an exemption applied where 'development that is reasonable and expected would not otherwise be possible'. This phrase was the subject of a dispute where retention of two regulated trees would require construction of bespoke building designs to accommodate the trees' location. It was argued that the additional expense of bespoke buildings would mean the development was not reasonable and expected. The court in that case confirmed that additional cost might be relevant, but found it had not been demonstrated by the evidence. Instead, the court focused on other factors,[23] concluding that the exemption was not satisfied in that case [44].

Also in South Australia, the Supreme Court considered tree protection provisions of the Planning and Development Act (SA) and found that, as a question of statutory interpretation, the legislative requirement that '[l]and should not be divided or developed where the division or development would be likely to result in a substantial tree-damaging activity occurring to a significant tree' would be effectively overridden if an exemption applied. In theory, this would include an existing exemption in favour of development in circumstances where 'it is demonstrated that all reasonable alternative development options and design solutions have been considered to prevent substantial tree-damaging activity occurring' [45].

By contrast, where the legislation clearly provides for protection of regulated trees without a development exemption, courts have found little difficulty in enforcing tree retention over development. For example, in the context of a proposed estate development, the ACT Civil and Administrative Tribunal considered legislation requiring the retention of significant vegetation, stating:

[22] The authors of this research go on to give a compelling discussion of the possible reasons for landowners' removal of trees on private land, in the absence of regulation.

[23] The other factors included the buildings' footprint, the capacity of the buildings to fit within normal building requirements, the possibility of being two storey, and the potential for making amendments to an 'off the shelf' design [at 110–114].

> An estate cannot be designed on a "blank canvas". It requires consideration of the legal, natural and physical constraints and opportunities that "run with the land". We see no difference in principle between an obligation to design movement networks that permit access for garbage trucks and an obligation to retain trees that constitute significant vegetation. This is not a new concept. Developers frequently encounter a feature or features of land that need to be retained, for legal or practical reasons, and take the feature or features into account when formulating a design.
>
> If a proponent regards the cost of retaining a tree as prohibitive or the prospects of successfully retaining it to be so low that it could not be sensibly attempted, the result is not to develop the area where the tree is sited [46, at 224–225]

This case also covered the topic of the loss of developer profits, with the Tribunal commenting 'we do not believe that retention of trees would cause a significant loss of profit, having regard to the increased amenity that the trees would bring' [46, at 423].

Considering different legislation with a similar effect, the Victorian Civil and Administrative Tribunal similarly found that not only should development take second place to retaining trees, but also that if the development was designed in a way that would eventually lead to a tree removal application, the development ought not to be allowed.[24]

Ultimately this is a choice of policy approach, as reflected in the applicable legislation and enforced by the courts, and means that when there is a clear conflict between development and tree protection, some jurisdictions provide for tree protections to take precedence whereas others allow for development to prevail.

2.5 Conclusion

This review has confirmed that there are several components that link together in each type of individual tree protection on private land. Each component presents differences across jurisdictions, and varying degrees of potential strength in application. I have presented these components in Table 2.3, by way of a simplified summary.

This Table 2.3 illustrates not only the wide variety of tree protection configurations, but also that a combination of weaknesses and strengths is likely to reduce the potential effectiveness of tree protections. Many of these components remain under-researched in terms of their application by councils and their impact on increasing canopy cover and other urban forest metrics. From this review, the key priority areas for further research are likely to be exclusions and exemptions, and enforcement in the context of approvals. Further research will be critical to inform the most effective ways to apply resources to increase urban forest across private land in Australia.

[24] *Czermak v Port Phillip City Council* [2006] VCAT 1987 [at 57] where the Tribunal predicted that the proposed development would create problems of light, leaf litter and perceived or real safety, and would ultimately lead to a request for removal of the tree(s) which the council would find difficult to resist.

Table 2.3 Summary of tree protection process components and the range of strength of protections

Process component	Range of protections	
	Weak <-------------------------------> Strong	
	Tree Registers	
Identifying trees	Minimal categories of significance Specifies pre-conditions By public nomination only Rarely updated High fees and costs No incentives for landowners	Several categories of significance No pre-conditions Proactive identification of trees Regularly updated Low fees and costs Valuable incentives for landowners
	Blanket Protections	
	Very high threshold criteria Only one criterion applicable	Low (or no) threshold criteria Three alternative criteria apply
Exclusions/ exemptions	Several categories of exemption Wide exemption criteria Policy favours development over tree retention	Few categories of exemption Narrow exemption criteria Policy favours tree retention over development
Enforcement (approvals)	High tree removal approval rate Low fees and costs	Low tree removal approval rate High fees and costs
Penalties	Low maximum penalties Low infringement fines	High maximum penalties High infringement fines
Enforcement (offences)	Infrequently enforced Only uses infringement fines No court prosecutions No deterrent factor applied	Regularly enforced Uses infringement fines Uses court prosecutions Deterrent factor often applied

References

1. Hurley J, Amati M, Deilami K, et al (2020) Where will all the trees be?—an assessment of urban forest cover and management for Australian cities. Prepared for Hort Innovation by the Centre for Urban Research, RMIT University, Melbourne
2. Ordóñez C (2021) Governance lessons from Australian local governments for retaining and protecting urban forests as nature based solutions. Nat-Based Solut 1:100004. https://doi.org/10.1016/j.nbsj.2021.100004
3. Clark C, Ordóñez C, Livesley SJ (2020) Private tree removal, public loss: Valuing and enforcing existing tree protection mechanisms is the key to retaining urban trees on private land. Landsc Urban Plan 203: 103899. https://doi.org/10.1016/j.landurbplan.2020.103899
4. Thorpe v Head, Transport for Victoria [2020] VSC 804
5. Pollard v Wilson [2010] NSWCA 68
6. National Trusts of Australia (2015) Significant tree protection: Understanding significance & the law. https://www.nationaltrust.org.au/wp-content/uploads/2016/06/Tree-Protection-in-Australia_National-Trusts-of-Australia.pdf. Accessed 12 Sep 2023
7. Faulds R (2020) Significant Tree Register. WESTERLY 65:72–75
8. Barker v Kyriakides [2007] NSWLEC 292
9. Lacey v City of Burnside [2009] SASC 136
10. Classic Constructions (Aust) Pty Ltd v Conservator of Flora and Fauna [2006] ACTSC 3
11. Silegna Pty Ltd v City of Burnside [2004] SAERDC 8
12. Australian Capital Territory Government (2023) Urban Forest Act 2023 (ACT)

13. Gorrey M (2021) More than 900 trees razed in Sydney's inner west under council policy. Sydney Morning Herald
14. City of Campbelltown v Genesis Equity (SA) Pty Ltd [2005] SAERDC 90
15. Government of Western Australia (2005) Planning and Development Act 2005 [WA]
16. Australian Capital Territory Government (2023) Urban Forest Bill 2022 (ACT) Revised Explanatory Statement. The Legislative Assembly for the Australian Capital Territory
17. Krajinovic v Heath [2018] TASSC 38
18. Taylor A (2023) "Difficult and expensive": Councils say laws don't deter illegal removal of trees. Sydney Morning Herald
19. Daniel C, Morrison TH, Phinn S (2016) The governance of private residential land in cities and spatial effects on tree cover. Environ Sci Policy 62:79–89. https://doi.org/10.1016/j.envsci.2016.01.015
20. Morgenroth J, O'Neil-Dunne J, Apiolaza LA (2017) Redevelopment and the urban forest: A study of tree removal and retention during demolition activities. Appl Geogr 82:1–10. https://doi.org/10.1016/j.apgeog.2017.02.011
21. Lensink M (2012) Tree protection laws in Australian states and territories. https://www.treenet.org/wp-content/uploads/2017/06/Urban-Trees_Lensink.pdf. Accessed 16 Jun 2023
22. Hall B, Blumenthal N (2023) Investigating options for tree protections on private land. https://walga.asn.au/getattachment/2023-WALGA-Urban-Forest-Conference-Content-Hub/Projects-Fall-Short-on-Canopy-Targets-as-Significa/213-104_12-15-12-35_HALL_BLUMENTHAL.pdf?lang=en-AU. Accessed 31 May 2023
23. City of Ballarat (2020) Exceptional Tree Register. https://www.ballarat.vic.gov.au/sites/default/files/2020-10/Exceptional%20Tree%20Register%20Information.pdf. Accessed 3 Nov 2023
24. Homewood Consulting Pty Ltd, City of Moonee Valley (2018) Moonee Valley City Council Significant Tree Review. City of Moonee Valley
25. Wyse SV, Beggs JR, Burns BR, Stanley MC (2015) Protecting trees at an individual level provides insufficient safeguard for urban forests. Landsc Urban Plan 141:112–122. https://doi.org/10.1016/j.landurbplan.2015.05.006
26. Hilbert DR, Koeser AK, Roman LA et al (2019) Development practices and ordinances predict inter-city variation in Florida urban tree canopy coverage. Landsc Urban Plan 190:103603. https://doi.org/10.1016/j.landurbplan.2019.103603
27. Belder RL, Delaporte KD, Caddy-Retalic S (2022) Urban tree protection in Australia: Review of regulatory matters. University of Adelaide, Adelaide
28. Morrison T, Wells J, Wilkins C (2021) Comparison of Australia's Tree Laws. Report prepared for the Conservation Council of South Australia
29. Scarmana G, McDougall K (2023) Assessing the relationship between tree dimensions in an urban environment. The International Archives of the Photogrammetry, Remote Sensing and Spatial Information Sciences XLVIII-1/W1-2023:437–442. https://doi.org/10.5194/isprs-archives-XLVIII-1-W1-2023-437-2023
30. Hargraves v City of Holdfast Bay [2018] SAERDC 41
31. Jarvis Property No 3 Pty Ltd v City of Holdfast Bay Assessment Panel [2023] SAERDC 2
32. Pace R, Masini E, Giuliarelli D, et al (2022) Tree measurements in the urban environment: Insights from traditional and digital field instruments to smartphone applications. Arboric Urban For 48:113–123. https://doi.org/10.48044/jauf.2022.009
33. Pearce L, Kirkpatrick J, Davison A (2013) Using size class distributions of species to deduce the dynamics of the private urban forest. Arboric Urban For 39. https://doi.org/10.48044/jauf.2013.011
34. Australian Capital Territory Government (2005) Tree Protection Act 2005 (ACT)
35. South Australian Parliament (2023) Inquiry into the Urban Forest—Interim Report
36. Ditara Pty Ltd v Corporation of the City of Norwood, Payneham & St Peters Assessment Manager [2022] SAERDC 19
37. Schneider R (2022) How Much Does An Arborist Report Cost? [2023]. In: hipages.com.au. https://hipages.com.au/article/how_much_does_an_arborist_report_cost. Accessed 30 Nov 2023

38. Greener Spaces Better Places (2014) Where are all the trees? An analysis of tree canopy cover in urban Australia. https://www.greenerspacesbetterplaces.com.au/media/163027/whereareallthetrees_report-final_rebranded_web.pdf. Accessed 31 May 2023
39. Amati M, Boruff B, Caccetta P, et al (2017) Where should all the trees go? Investigating the impact of tree canopy cover on socio-economic status and wellbeing in LGAs. prepared for Hort Innovation by the Centre for Urban Research, RMIT University, Melbourne, Australia
40. Hill E, Dorfman JH, Kramer E (2010) Evaluating the impact of government land use policies on tree canopy coverage. Land Use Policy 27:407–414. https://doi.org/10.1016/j.landusepol.2009.05.007
41. Croeser T, Ordóñez C, Threlfall C et al (2020) Patterns of tree removal and canopy change on public and private land in the City of Melbourne. Sustain Cities Soc 56:102096. https://doi.org/10.1016/j.scs.2020.102096
42. Kronenberg J, Łaszkiewicz E, Sziło J (2021) Voting with one's chainsaw: What happens when people are given the opportunity to freely remove urban trees? Landsc Urban Plan 209:104041. https://doi.org/10.1016/j.landurbplan.2021.104041
43. City of Nedlands (2022) Local Planning Scheme No. 3, Amendment No. 12. City of Nedlands, Nedlands
44. Savoy Developments Pty Ltd v Town of Gawler [2013] SAERDC 32
45. Staikopolous v City of West Torrens [2016] SASC 183
46. Village No 22 Pty Ltd v ACT Planning and Land Authority [2021] ACAT 43
47. Sheehan v Santosa [2023] NSWLEC 1279
48. Corporation of the City of Unley v Crichton (No2) [2019] SAERDC 43

Chapter 3
Protecting Forested Areas

Abstract Forested areas on private urban land are uncommon because of past extensive land clearing and urban landscape fragmentation. Most of the literature on private forested areas has focused on large, non-urban landholdings. Nevertheless, the same protective mechanisms may apply to urban land, and some literature has considered their application to peri-urban land. Broadly, the types of regulatory mechanism for protection of forested areas are by way of covenant or by the imposition and enforcement of land use restrictions. Conservation covenants are an agreement to preserve and manage a land area for conservation. These agreements are permanent and arguably reduce the economic value of the land. In Australia, conservation covenants are not well used, even where tax benefits may result. The other type of mechanism is where land use is restricted for reasons relevant to the particular forested area. These include the protection of biodiversity, the protection of native vegetation and the protection of cultural or natural heritage. Biodiversity protections apply where threatened species or ecosystems are at risk. Native vegetation is subject to statutory prohibitions on unauthorised clearing in all states and territories. Protection of natural or cultural heritage includes forested areas and trees, and is particularly relevant to the protection of Indigenous heritage values.

3.1 Introduction

Internationally, conservation on private land is seen as a necessary part of the solution to biodiversity loss, with research in this area rapidly increasing [1] and particularly focused on four countries, including the USA and Australia [2]. The application of conservation mechanisms to existing forested areas is a key topic in understanding how and why conservation on private land can be effective. Most of the literature considers private land conservation in the context of large landholdings, usually rural, which extend to thousands of hectares and where the landowners face issues such as problematic leasehold terms, competing mining interests and the need to derive an income from the property [3, 4]. By contrast, the application of the same conservation mechanisms to smaller, urban landholdings is rarely addressed. This is most likely

E. J. Scaife, *Urban Tree Protection on Private Land*,
SpringerBriefs in Law, https://doi.org/10.1007/978-981-95-1857-9_3

due to the lack of forested areas in the urban environment, resulting from historic fragmentation and land clearing already undertaken in those areas.

However, in Australia, peri-urban land (land on the boundary between rural and urban areas) can contain tracts of forested areas, albeit on smaller landholdings, and some literature has started to address the application of private land conservation mechanisms to these peri-urban landholdings in Australia [3, 5]. Private urban or peri-urban forested land can be used to support conservation areas and strategies by buffering protected areas, providing linkages in a fragmented landscape, containing urban areas by protecting peri-urban forests from development, and by supporting and protecting specific threatened species or ecosystems (all ideally as part of a broader scale bioregional plan) [5]. These uses can be valuable in conservation efforts, and the mechanisms for harnessing them are essentially the same as for larger areas of forested land. In the urban environment, forested areas can provide much-needed recreational spaces as well as serving conservation purposes, but this dual use can be controversial and, in any event, is most often applicable where the land is publicly owned.[1]

As urban or peri-urban forested areas tend to be smaller than rural landholdings, this also gives rise to a higher likelihood of problems with degradation, a lack of high ecological values and greater management effort required to support ecosystem processes. In addition, higher economic land value (or potential value) due to the possibility of urban development arguably reduces landowner motivation to engage in conservation measures [3] and, quite possibly, adds to the attraction of clearing the land in advance of potential sale [6].

The primary types of mechanism for protecting forested areas on private urban land are through conservation covenants and by way of land use restrictions. There are other statutory-based mechanisms available or foreseeable, but most of these are not yet well-used in urban areas or are used in conjunction with conservation covenants. These alternative mechanisms are discussed briefly in the final section of this chapter.

3.2 Conservation Covenants

3.2.1 Conservation Covenants in Australia

In property law, a covenant is a 'promise contained in a deed to land or real estate which is binding upon the current owner and all future owners. It defines the limitations, conditions or restrictions on the use of that land' [7]. These are known as restrictive covenants and have been legally recognised in Australia for over 150 years [8]. A *conservation* covenant is a specific type of covenant where the underlying promise is a voluntary agreement made between a landholder and an authorised

[1] See, for example, a study carried out on conservation easements in the San Francisco Bay Area [52].

body that aims to protect and enhance the natural, cultural and/or scientific values of certain land [7]. Conservation covenants are a more recent variation of covenant and were first introduced in 1970. Since then, legislation establishing conservation covenants has been enacted by the Commonwealth and by each state and territory of Australia.[2]

In 2019, there were almost 4,900 conservation covenants in place across Australia, covering approximately 4.5 million hectares [4]. By way of comparison, in the USA the equivalent mechanism of conservation easements is estimated to cover 40 million acres (16.2 million hectares) [9].

3.2.2 *Permanence*

The permanence of a conservation covenant is a key factor in the strength of this conservation mechanism. Conservation covenants are registered on the deed or land title, making them binding on future owners of the land. Ordinarily this applies in perpetuity (or for the life of the lease in relation to leasehold land), but some conservation covenants allow for a shorter time period (e.g. 25 years) or allow the covenant to be revocable by the landowner in certain circumstances. A 2017 study of data on covenant releases indicated that, where the covenant could be revoked by a single party, this happened in 19% of cases, usually at the instigation of the landowner. By contrast, where revocation could only occur with the agreement of multiple parties, usually including a government Minister, the rate of release was only 0.12% [10].

Conservation covenants have been utilised by private conservation organisations to protect areas of private land either permanently as part of a property acquisition program, or as part of a rolling fund to purchase properties of high ecological value, create a conservation covenant over the land and then re-sell the land with the new encumbrance permanently on the title. In the latter case, the new purchaser of the land may be selected to be sympathetic to the conservation of the land.

Conservation covenants are also used in conjunction with development conditions involving offsets or subdivision. The covenant can provide a permanent legal barrier to any proposed undoing of the conservation measures undertaken in exchange for development permission. The case law on conservation covenants often relates to the disputes around the use of covenants in these types of exchanges, both where the

[2] For a summary of the relevant legislation, see Fitzsimons [4], Table 2, Covenanting programs in Australian jurisdictions and primary legislation.

landowner objects to the imposed condition[3] or where development has been refused despite the landowner offering a covenant.[4]

3.2.3 Ongoing Management and Monitoring

The ongoing management of the land for conservation purposes is an important consideration. Conservation covenants usually comprise a combination of both restrictive and positive obligations, since they essentially establish a partnership arrangement for ongoing conservation of the specified land which transfers to new successive landowners. The motivations, resources and skills of the parties are the subject of a number of studies in both Australia and the USA.

Monitoring of conservation covenants is important not only for compliance and measuring ecological outcomes, but also to inform adaptive management practices over time, particularly in the context of managing biodiversity conservation plans for climate change impacts [11–13]. There are difficulties associated with monitoring conservation covenants, partly due to the limited resources of covenanting organisations [14]. This may be assisted in future by using geospatial data [15] and photo monitoring to track changes over time and at different scales [16].

3.2.4 Change in Land Value

Conservation covenants arguably reduce the value of the land or make a sale more difficult by reducing the number of potential buyers in the market [3]. They can also limit the productive value of the land by restricting the types of activities a landowner can carry out on the land. These financial impacts can act as a disincentive to landowners considering establishing a conservation covenant, particularly those whose income is derived from the land or who intend to sell the land for financial gain.

The potential negative financial impacts of entering conservation covenants may be balanced by the provision of financial incentives such as biodiversity offset payments, stewardship payments and tax incentives or rates rebates [17]. However, the effectiveness of tax incentives has been questioned in view of the continued slow uptake of conservation covenants following the introduction of tax incentives in 2001 [3]. In the USA, the widespread use of financial incentives in relation to the equivalent mechanism of conservation easements has been criticised for tending to protect land

[3] *Reid v Western Australian Planning Commission* [53] discusses the power of the Western Australian Planning Commission to impose a condition of subdivision that a permanent conservation covenant be granted over a portion of the land.

[4] See *Phelps v Development Consent Authority* [21] regarding a refused subdivision proposal; and *Mackenzie Architects International Pty Ltd v Ku-ring-gai Council* [54] regarding a refused biobanking offset proposal.

of lower ecological value where exactly the opposite is needed [18], and giving rise to a lack of landowner motivation to engage in proper long term conservation management of the land. Similarly, giving development rights (such as the right to subdivide) or mining rights in exchange for conservation covenants may mean the covenant is the result of strategic investment decision rather than a predominantly charitable conservation motivation, negatively impacting the longer-term management of the covenant [1].

A 2022 study of landowner preferences for conservation covenant incentives found that incentives for initial participation in a covenant were not as sought-after as assistance for ongoing management of a covenant. The authors noted a widespread preference for land rates rebates, above (but not necessarily exclusive of) other types of financial assistance [17].

3.2.5 Effectiveness of Conservation Covenants

Longer term achievement of biodiversity conservation outcomes on covenanted land has been difficult to research due to limited collection of ecological monitoring data [10, 14, 19]. However, one factor emerging as a potential policy issue is the motivation of successive landowners, who take on the obligations and restrictions associated with a covenant but may not be motivated by the same conservation values as the original covenantor [20]. This is seen as a potential causal factor leading to breaches or releases from conservation covenants [10]. Another emerging threat is the interference by third parties trespassing on the land and causing damage to the ecological values of the land, such as, for example, by removing timber [10].

Probably the highest value use of conservation covenants is where the landowner is a private non-government conservation organisation and has the resources and support to retain, protect and manage the land permanently for conservation. In those cases, although the creation of a conservation covenant may be seen as superfluous, it nevertheless adds a legal strength to the protection of the land and can allow for ongoing support by governments and conservation agencies.[5]

In a case concerning a proposed exchange of conservation covenant for subdivision rights, the Northern Territory Court of Appeal upheld the original decision to refuse the proposed exchange, which had been made partly on the basis that the use of planning restrictions was likely to be more effective than conservation covenants. The reasons for this were, broadly, that the planning scheme requirements were clear, known and well established, and there was a duty imposed on the Minister and the Development Consent Authority to enforce the planning scheme. By contrast, the

[5] Even when operating at their highest, in Australia conservation covenants will only apply to the extent of the landowner's title, which normally does not extend to sub-surface mineral resources. Thus, conservation covenants will still remain subject to sub-surface mining interests. This issue is more likely to impact larger and more remote landholdings (and has caused the loss of conservation covenants in some cases), but in theory this potential conflict remains applicable to urban or peri-urban areas.

court found the terms of the conservation covenants were unclear, there was no duty on any authority or Minister to enforce the covenants, and any enforcement may be subject to political or public interest considerations [21].

3.3 Land Use Restrictions

3.3.1 Land Use Zoning

Statutory-based land use restrictions apply in all Australian jurisdictions. The initial control over land use in urban and peri-urban areas is in the form of zoning; that is a planning framework where state/territory and local governments together create a regional planning scheme that includes an allowable use for all land areas within a local government area. This zoned use becomes the starting point for development applications that may be made by landholders. In peri-urban areas, a zoned use change from rural to urban can increase the economic value of the land. Normally, land zoned as urban will also specify the allowable housing density. This is important because population density and the proximity to urban areas are key drivers of the change from native vegetation to urban land use [22].

Landholders may still need to apply for approval to develop and/or clear their land in accordance with the zoned use. Where land contains a forested area, it may be protected from clearing or land use change based on particular reasons relevant to that land area. These reasons include the protection of native vegetation, the protection of biodiversity (particular species or ecosystems), and the protection of cultural or natural heritage.

3.3.2 Native Vegetation Clearing Restrictions

The clearing of native vegetation on a private landholding may be subject to regulation additional to development approval. Restrictions on clearing native vegetation have been legislated in all states and territories.[6] The restrictions essentially work by requiring permission to clear native vegetation and creating an offence if clearing occurs without authorisation. Assessment of clearing permit applications are typically the responsibility of the relevant state/territory government, or a specific authorising body.

Historically, this represents a reversal of government attitudes prevailing when rural land was initially sold. Many original sale or lease contracts specifically required the landowner to undertake clearing of the land as a condition of the sale, as this was

[6] NSW has separate controls for clearing in rural and non-rural areas [55], with urban areas included in the latter; all other jurisdictions apply the same legislation to both urban and rural areas. For a discussion of the various legislative controls applicable, see GM Bates [26], Chapter 7.

seen as necessary in order to enable income production from the land. Enforcement of native vegetation controls have thus led to complaints from landowners that their land is no longer able to be used for income producing purposes. For example, the following extract, from an unsuccessful claim by a NSW landowner, sets out the impact said to be experienced:

> [Mr Spencer] claims the prohibitions, including a refusal of permission to clear a large amount of vegetation on his property in 2007, resulted in his property being assessed by the State's Rural Assistance Authority as commercially unviable. He claims this assessment, together with the fact that he was unable to pursue a number of projects on the property which would have necessitated land clearing, ultimately or eventually led to the property being sold by the mortgagees. In simple terms, he claims that but for the existence and effect of the NSW vegetation clearance laws, he would still be on his property Saarahnlee and would be well advanced on a number of different and financially productive projects (either alone or in conjunction with other investors) such as wind farming, fine merino production and trout farming. Instead, he claims he is without a home at all, and financially ruined [23, para 11]

In the peri-urban context, landowners are more likely to be interested in financial gains resulting from urban development rather than relying upon the land for income. Nevertheless, a similar conflict can arise in peri-urban areas where a landowner is unable to realise an anticipated gain due to the application of clearing restrictions. Provision for compensation resulting from the imposition of land use restrictions, including native vegetation clearing restrictions, is not generally provided by state/territory governments [24]. In the example above, Mr Spencer attempted legally to link Australia's national environmental obligations to state native vegetation clearing controls in order to trigger Commonwealth compensation, but was unsuccessful [23, 24].

There are usually a number of exemptions that may apply to exempt a landowner from the requirement to obtain a clearing permit. Exemptions tend to be for smaller areas and specific purposes, such as mending fences or track maintenance. Other exemptions apply where the clearing is required under different legislation, such as fire hazard reduction for bushfire protection. Bushfire protection allowances are a particular source of contention due to the effect of undermining native vegetation protection measures, as they may allow specified clearance of trees and vegetation around residences without requiring a permit and with only a loose connection to bushfire risk [25].

3.3.3 Biodiversity Protections

Australia has a series of legislated protections for threatened species of flora, fauna and ecosystems, enacted in both state/territory and federal jurisdictions. These controls can apply to protect trees or forested areas on private land where the trees themselves are protected flora, or are a part of a protected ecosystem, or provide habitat or food source for a threatened species of fauna. Land clearing may also be identified as a threatening process to a particular species [26].

3.3.3.1 Local Protections

In some jurisdictions, larger scale plans such as bioregional biodiversity or environmental plans form part of the planning controls applicable to private land, typically administered by local government. For example, in Victoria there are bioregional areas identified across the state [27] and local planning tools include the use of overlays to support specific environmental purposes, such as the protection of specified threatened ecosystems. A number of these overlays either directly or indirectly support the retention of trees on private land in urban areas by providing additional local controls for tree removal within identified geographical areas that are based on larger scale biodiversity plans covering both public and private land [28].

3.3.3.2 State/Territory Protections

All states and territories have statutory procedures for environmental impact assessment of certain development proposals. Environmental impact assessment is a decision-support tool: a way of ensuring that environmental impacts are reviewed and reported as part of the development decision making process, so that environmental impacts can be considered alongside social and economic impacts. Each state and territory has separate legislation for environmental impact assessment. However, all require a certain level of significance of likely environmental impact to trigger the assessment requirement. Typically, the assessed impacts include (where appropriate) biodiversity impacts, such as impacts on threatened species or ecological communities, and native vegetation loss. Environmental impact assessments, although not binding on a decision-maker, can result in additional protections for urban trees and forests by influencing a decision to refuse the proposed development, or to include certain conditions on approval that are designed to remove, reduce or mitigate the foreseen environmental impacts.[7] However, the effectiveness of environmental impact assessment in the Australian context has been questioned on the basis that it can be used to support politically biased development decisions, rather than as an evidence-based, scientific decision-support tool [29].

3.3.3.3 National Protections

Where an 'action'[8] is likely to have a significant impact on a matter of national environmental significance, it may be referred for federal environmental impact assessment. Clearing of vegetation or removal of trees may constitute such an action, as it may be a threatening process to a species or ecosystem of national environmental

[7] For a detailed review of the state and territory environmental impact assessment procedures, see GM Bates' textbook *Environmental Law in Australia* [26].

[8] Section 523 of the *EPBC Act 1999 (Cth)* [31] defines an action as including a project, development, undertaking, activity, or series of activities, or an alteration to any of those things.

significance. In peri-urban areas this has potential to apply, for example, to the banksia woodlands remaining in the peri-urban areas surrounding Perth. These woodlands are listed as a threatened ecological community under the *EPBC Act 1999 (Cth)* [30, 31], where the greatest threat to the woodlands is clearing, including clearing due to urban development [32]. However, the small and fragmented land areas typically involved in peri-urban clearing or development applications may be difficult to characterise individually as constituting a significant impact. Whilst an approach considering cumulative impacts may address this issue, Australia has less cumulative impact legal coverage at the national level than other common law jurisdictions [33] and the operation of national legislation has been criticised for considering impacts in isolation and thus underestimating cumulative impacts [34–36].

3.3.3.4 Biodiversity Offsets

The use of offsets to mitigate the impacts of development on biodiversity is increasing [37]. Biodiversity offsetting is a complex topic and requires careful consideration of whether it is justified at all, whether equivalence exists between the offset and the loss, and the certainty of the proposed offsets outcome [38]. The Commonwealth State of the Environment Report (2021) referred to the concerning use of offsets to protect biodiversity from development impacts, commenting on the lack of successful outcomes and inadequate oversight [37]. In peri-urban areas the use of biodiversity offsets has been particularly criticised for exacerbating the problems associated with biodiversity loss by effectively relocating nature away from residents, leading to arguments that offsets ought to be restricted to land areas within a specified proximity to the impact site [39].

3.4 Other Mechanisms

In general, the suite of mechanisms for private land conservation in urban areas are neither well researched [40] nor well known [41]. Existing alternative mechanism for protecting private forested areas include:

- Stands of trees identified individually may be included in individual tree protections, as noted in Chap. 2.
- Public acquisition of private land for conservation purposes, particularly where land areas have been identified as having very high ecological value. This is discussed in Chap. 6.
- Private reserves in Australia may be formally established under conservation programs such as Private Wildlife Sanctuaries or Private Protected Areas and supported by the National Reserve System [42]. Around 6% of the National Reserve System is made up of privately owned land. This requires the protected area to be 'conserved forever, with effective legal means guaranteeing its perpetual

conservation' [43]. 'Legal means' includes conservation covenants and extends to contracts and agreements that may not fulfil the criteria of a covenant [4].
- Legislation designed to preserve or protect natural or cultural heritage, which normally covers specific trees or trees occurring within heritage areas. These protections apply at both state/territory and federal levels. For example, declarations may be sought for the preservation or protection of trees of particular significance for Aboriginal heritage under the *Aboriginal and Torres Strait Islander Heritage Protection Act 1984 (Cth)* [44, 45].
- Land use or management in accordance with statutory-based carbon and biodiversity market instruments. These types of instruments are generally regarded as applying to larger, non-urban landholdings, with a focus on land rehabilitation. In particular, the *Nature Repair Act 2023 (Cth)* establishes a framework for a national biodiversity market [46], but the design details and likelihood of success remain unclear [47].

Literature on future statutory-based mechanisms that may support urban forest protection on private land in Australia is coalescing around introducing a general statutory duty of care to the environment. The UK has already introduced a statutory form of this duty of care and Australia's legal system recognises other types of legally enforceable duty of care, both with and without a statutory basis [26].

3.5 Conclusion

There is limited literature on the use and effectiveness of private land conservation mechanisms in urban or peri-urban areas. These areas differ from larger rural landholdings due to the likelihood of being zoned for urban development, pre-existing fragmentation and degradation issues, land ownership comprising larger numbers of individually owned smaller land parcels, and land being adjacent to higher human population densities. Although occasionally resulting in positive benefits for conservation, in general these characteristics tend to create additional problems for the successful preservation of forested areas on private land. This is not only in relation to the mechanisms described above, but also the operation of other drivers and incentives on landholders, such as land tax, where the implications may not always be apparent [48].

For these reasons, it is critical to understand the reasons for urban landowners' interest and participation in conservation measures [49], yet these are under-researched components [2, 5]. Landowner engagement in private land conservation was examined in a systematic literature review, concluding with the key message that communication and trust are critical elements [1, 50]. Where financial drivers counter conservation aims, and government assistance depends upon the relinquishment of property rights as well as taking on legally enforceable obligations, it is perhaps understandable that there may be more interest in voluntary non-binding arrangements than participation in regulatory mechanisms [40]. Having said that, landowners may appreciate the 'peace of mind that the land will remain protected, even if the property changes hands' [51] that comes with conservation covenants.

References

1. Gooden J, 't Sas-Rolfes M (2020) A review of critical perspectives on private land conservation in academic literature. Ambio 49:1019–1034. https://doi.org/10.1007/s13280-019-01258-y
2. Cortés Capano G, Toivonen T, Soutullo A, Di Minin E (2019) The emergence of private land conservation in scientific literature: a review. Biol Conserv 237:191–199. https://doi.org/10.1016/j.biocon.2019.07.010
3. England P (2015) Conservation covenants: Are they working and what have we learned? Univ Tasman Law Rev 34:92–110
4. Fitzsimons JA (2015) Private protected areas in Australia: current status and future directions. Nat Conserv 10:1–23. https://doi.org/10.3897/natureconservation.10.8739
5. Crossman ND, Bryan BA, Ostendorf B, Collins S (2007) Systematic landscape restoration in the rural–urban fringe: Meeting conservation planning and policy goals. Biodivers Conserv 16:3781–3802. https://doi.org/10.1007/s10531-007-9180-8
6. Kronenberg J, Łaszkiewicz E, Sziło J (2021) Voting with one's chainsaw: What happens when people are given the opportunity to freely remove urban trees? Landsc Urban Plan 209:104041. https://doi.org/10.1016/j.landurbplan.2021.104041
7. Department of Climate Change, Energy, the Environment and Water. Conservation covenants. Australian Government. https://www.dcceew.gov.au/environment/biodiversity/conservation/covenants
8. Tooher J (1992) Restrictive covenants and public planning legislation—should the landowner feel touched and concerned? Environ Plan Law J 2:63
9. US Endowment for Forestry and Communities (2017) National Conservation Easement Database. https://site.tplgis.org/NCED/storymap/index.html
10. Hardy MJ, Fitzsimons JA, Bekessy SA, Gordon A (2017) Exploring the permanence of conservation covenants. Conserv Lett 10:221–230. https://doi.org/10.1111/conl.12243
11. Rissman AR, Owley J, Shaw MR, Thompson B (Buzz) (2015) Adapting conservation easements to climate change. Conserv Lett 8:68–76. https://doi.org/10.1111/conl.12099
12. Owley J, Cheever F, Rissman AR et al (2018) Climate change challenges for land conservation: Rethinking conservation easements, strategies, and tools. Denver Law Rev 95:727–779
13. Rissman A, Bihari M, Hamilton C et al (2013) Land management restrictions and options for change in perpetual conservation easements. Environ Manage 52:277–288. https://doi.org/10.1007/s00267-013-0091-z
14. Fitzsimons JA, Ben CC (2014) Conservation covenants on private land: Issues with measuring and achieving biodiversity outcomes in Australia. Environ Manage 54:606–616. https://doi.org/10.1007/s00267-014-0329-4
15. Rissman AR, Owley J, L'Roe AW, et al (2017) Public access to spatial data on private-land conservation. Ecol Soc 22:art24. https://doi.org/10.5751/ES-09330-220224
16. Rissman AR, Reiner R, Merenlender AM (2007) Monitoring natural resources on rangeland conservation easements: Who's minding the easement? Rangelands 29:21–26. https://doi.org/10.2111/1551-501X(2007)29[21:MNRORC]2.0.CO;2
17. Selinske MJ, Howard N, Fitzsimons JA, et al (2022) "Splitting the bill" for conservation: Perceptions and uptake of financial incentives by landholders managing privately protected areas. Conserv Sci Pract 4:n/a. https://doi.org/10.1111/csp2.12660
18. Hansen AJ, Mullan K, Theobald DM, et al (2022) Informing conservation decisions to target private lands of highest ecological value and risk of loss. Ecol Appl 32. https://doi.org/10.1002/eap.2612

19. Kiesecker JM, Comendant T, Grandmason T et al (2007) Conservation easements in context: A quantitative analysis of their use by the nature conservancy. Front Ecol Environ 5:125–130. https://doi.org/10.1890/1540-9295(2007)5[125:CEICAQ]2.0.CO;2
20. Rissman AR, Kazer A, DeMets C, Martell E (2023) Sustaining land and people over time: Relationships with successor landowners on conservation easements. People Nat (Hoboken) 5:542–556. https://doi.org/10.1002/pan3.10436
21. Phelps v Development Consent Authority [2012] NTCA 2
22. Vijayan A, Maina JM, Lawson R et al (2021) Land use planning to support climate change adaptation in threatened plant communities. J Environ Manage 298:113533. https://doi.org/10.1016/j.jenvman.2021.113533
23. Spencer v Commonwealth [2015] FCA 754
24. Finlay L (2016) Environmentally sensitive areas in Western Australia: highlighting the limits of the "just terms" guarantee. Univ West Aust Law Rev 41:49
25. Salgo M, Gillespie J (2018) Cracking the Code: A legal geography and political ecological perspective on vegetation clearing regulations. Aust Geogr 49:483–496. https://doi.org/10.1080/00049182.2018.1440688
26. Bates GM (2023) Environmental law in Australia, 11th edn. LexisNexis Butterworths, Sydney
27. Victoria State Government Bioregions and EVC benchmarks. In: https://www.environment.vic.gov.au/biodiversity/bioregions-and-evc-benchmarks
28. Victoria State Government (2017) Planning for Biodiversity. https://www.environment.vic.gov.au/__data/assets/pdf_file/0014/91220/Planning-for-biodiversity-Guidance.pdf. Accessed 19 Apr 2025
29. Bond A, Pope J, Fundingsland M, et al (2020) Explaining the political nature of environmental impact assessment (EIA): A neo-Gramscian perspective. J Clean Prod 244:118694. https://doi.org/10.1016/j.jclepro.2019.118694
30. Ritchie AL, Svejcar LN, Ayre BM et al (2021) Corrigendum to: A threatened ecological community: Research advances and priorities for Banksia woodlands. Aust J Bot 69:111. https://doi.org/10.1071/BT20089_CO
31. Australian Government (1999) Environment Protection and Biodiversity Conservation Act 1999 (Cth). Australia
32. Australian Government (2016) Approved Conservation Advice (incorporating listing advice) for the Banksia Woodlands of the Swan Coastal Plain ecological community
33. Nelson R, Shirley LM (2023) The latent potential of cumulative effects concepts in National and International Environmental Impact Assessment Regimes. Transnatl Environ Law 12:150–174. https://doi.org/10.1017/S2047102522000243
34. Samuel G (2020) Independent Review of the EPBC Act: Final report
35. Thomas H, Ward MS, Simmonds JS et al (2024) Poor compliance and exemptions facilitate ongoing deforestation. Conserv Biol. https://doi.org/10.1111/cobi.14354
36. Reside AE, Cosgrove AJ, Pointon R et al (2019) How to send a finch extinct. Environ Sci Policy 94:163–173. https://doi.org/10.1016/j.envsci.2019.01.005
37. Cresswell ID, Janke T, Johnston EL (2021) Australia State of the Environment 2021: Overview. Independent report to the Australian Government Minister for the Environment. Canberra
38. Preston B (2016) Biodiversity offsets: adequacy and efficacy in theory and practice. Environ Plan Law J 33:93
39. Kalliolevo H, Gordon A, Sharma R, et al (2021) Biodiversity offsetting can relocate nature away from people: An empirical case study in Western Australia. Conserv Sci Pract 3. https://doi.org/10.1111/csp2.512
40. Eon C, Breadsell J, Byrne J, Morrison G (2020) How can urban development support biodiversity retention on private lands? Low Carbon Living CRC
41. Bennett DE, Pejchar L, Romero B et al (2018) Using practitioner knowledge to expand the toolbox for private lands conservation. Biol Conserv 227:152–159. https://doi.org/10.1016/j.biocon.2018.09.003
42. Kamal S, Grodzińska-Jurczak M, Brown G (2015) Conservation on private land: A review of global strategies with a proposed classification system. J Environ Planning Manage 58:576–597. https://doi.org/10.1080/09640568.2013.875463

43. Australian Government (2023) National Reserve System protected area requirements. In: Department of Climate Change, Energy, the Environment and Water. https://www.dcceew.gov.au/environment/land/nrs/about-nrs/requirements. Accessed 19 Apr 2025
44. Clark v Minister for the Environment [2019] FCA 2027
45. Onus v Minister for the Environment [2020] FCA 1807
46. Australian Government (2025) Nature repair market. In: Department of Climate Change, Energy, the Environment and Water. https://www.dcceew.gov.au/environment/environmental-markets/nature-repair-market. Accessed 19 Apr 2025
47. O'Connor P (2023) Can the government's new market mechanism help save nature? Yes—if we get the devil out of the detail. The Conversation. https://theconversation.com/can-the-governments-new-market-mechanism-help-save-nature-yes-if-we-get-the-devil-out-of-the-detail-218713
48. Stokes R (2005) Environmental implications of land taxes on principal places of residence. Local Government Law Journal 11:37–47
49. Uebel K, Rhodes J, Wilson KA, Dean AJ (2021) Environmental management in the peri-urban region: Psychological and contextual factors influencing private land conservation actions. Environ Manage 68:184–197. https://doi.org/10.1007/s00267-021-01487-6
50. Tanguay L, Bissonnette J-F, Turgeon K, Calmé S (2021) Intervention levers for increasing social acceptance of conservation measures on private land: A systematic literature review and comprehensive typology. Environ Res Lett 16:073007. https://doi.org/10.1088/1748-9326/ac0d79
51. Trust for Nature (Victoria) (2024) Conservation covenants. In: https://trustfornature.org.au/what-we-do/conservation-covenants
52. Rissman AR, Merenlender AM (2008) The conservation contributions of conservation easements: Analysis of the San Francisco bay area protected lands spatial database. Ecol Soc 13:34
53. Reid v Western Australian Planning Commission [2016] WASCA 181
54. Mackenzie Architects International Pty Ltd v Ku-ring-gai Council [2015] NSWLEC 1353
55. NSW Government (2017) State Environmental Planning Policy (Vegetation in Non-Rural Areas) 2017 [NSW]

Chapter 4
Providing Space for Trees

Abstract Planning controls regulating the footprint of built form in urban development exist across Australia. For the most part, they relate to aesthetic and privacy values. They take the form of specified percentages limiting building footprint, impervious surfaces and/or setback measurements from boundary lines. Landscaping requirements, which relate to aesthetic and also environmental values, also exist and often specify the inclusion of deep soil areas designed to support different sizes of tree. These planning mechanisms are an indirect way to influence the likelihood that trees and other plantings will grow in and around redevelopments and new developments. Urban design solutions and the loss of the Australian backyard are the two areas where literature has coalesced. There is fierce agreement that private gardens are in decline and that the two proximate causes are urban infill (in older suburbs) and the construction of larger houses on smaller plots in new developments. The reduced and reducing urban green space is a complex problem and may require a range of planning and regulatory responses to alter the current trajectory.

4.1 Introduction

There is little doubt that the private open space in Australia's urban areas has reduced over the past 50 years and is continuing to reduce. This phenomenon has been documented with the aid of aerial and satellite imagery in research using localised case study areas to provide examples of this Australia-wide issue [1–4]. The consequence of the continuous reduction in private open space, which is the area usually used for private gardens, is a reduction in urban greenery (and particularly trees) on private land. If this reduction trend continues unabated, a point will eventually be reached where urban forest can no longer exist on private land.

The available research reveals some consistency in general findings. The main finding is that housing density is negatively correlated with the area of private open space. In other words, as housing density increases, private open space decreases. Land parcel size is also correlated with the area of private open space: the smaller the land parcel, the smaller the area of private open space [2].

E. J. Scaife, *Urban Tree Protection on Private Land*,
SpringerBriefs in Law, https://doi.org/10.1007/978-981-95-1857-9_4

4.2 Land Parcel and Building Size

4.2.1 *Trends Over Time*

Australian building and land statistics show trends over time for smaller urban land parcel sizes. According to the Australian Bureau of Statistics, in 2022 the most common size range of residential land parcels in major urban areas was 600 to 800 m^2. By contrast, the majority of *new* dwellings used less than 400 m^2 of land [5].

These reductions in land parcel size are not matched by an equivalent reduction in building size. Most Australian housing consists of private, detached dwellings. The average floor area of new detached dwellings in Australia rose steadily from around 100 m^2 in 1950 [6], to 167 m^2 in 1983 [7], to 229.1 m^2 in 2001, and has remained at a similar level ever since, subject to a peak in 2009 of 245.9 m^2, when Australian houses were proclaimed to be the largest in the world [8, 9]. Recent statistics show the average new house floor area at 232.3 m^2 in 2021–22 [8]. These measurements exclude outdoor spaces.

Historic aerial and land use data has provided evidence of the reduction in private open space beginning at least 50 years ago, with one Melbourne study documenting the trend beginning with new homes constructed in the 1950s [2, 3]. Prior to this change, there is evidence that the trend was the opposite: canopy cover in private open space was increasing [2]. In broad terms, the percentage of a residential land parcel occupied by built form has shifted from around 30% pre-1950 to more than 50% [2]. A study comparing urban infill sites pre- and post- infill development showed impervious surface area had increased from an average of 28.4% to 59.7% of parcel area [4]. For interest, the calculation of percentage of floor area based on the current statistical averages gives a similar result of floor area comprising 58.1% of site area. If outdoor impervious surfaces were included, this percentage would be higher.

These trends are apparent in both urban infill (or urban consolidation) and in new developments on the urban fringe. On the urban fringe, the change is more rapid and stark, as it involves many, sometimes hundreds, of new houses being constructed within the same land area over a brief time period, with the majority exhibiting the same traits as noted above [10]. Often called 'urban sprawl' this type of development sometimes has the additional environmental impact of being immediately preceded by comprehensive clearing of native vegetation (see Chap. 3). By contrast, urban infill tends to happen in a 'piecemeal' fashion, incrementally and over longer periods of time.

4.2.2 *Underlying Causes*

Research into the reasons for these trends has produced a wide variety of suggested underlying causes. It is a complex area for research because there are many interconnected factors, and it is difficult to pinpoint any single factor as being the key underlying cause of the reducing garden space. Tony Hall's book '*The Life and Death of the Australian Backyard*' [3] published in 2010, remains the key work in this area. The main reasons put forward by Hall and others include:

- The persistence of the "Australian dream" of owning a large, detached home [3, 11];
- A preference for internal home space over garden space, whether for lifestyle [3], status [9, 12] or investment [13] reasons;
- A lack of effective regulation, in particular regulation aimed at preserving garden space [3]
- A lack of developer incentives to retain and improve residential garden space [11, 14];
- The economic drivers resulting from a process for new development whereby developers sell the land parcels, but individual owners are then responsible for the design and construction of a new residence (as opposed to developers also constructing the dwellings) [3];
- The economic reality that square-shaped single storey dwellings are cheaper to construct than irregular shaped or two storey dwellings [3]; and
- An assumed reliance on the use of cars for transport, supporting urban expansion beyond the reach of existing urban transport systems [15] and necessitating car parking, driveways and crossovers in new residences [3, 4].

There does not appear to be agreement on any single cause apart from, perhaps, a lack of effective regulation. Even this factor involves divergent perspectives arriving at the same conclusion. For example, there is the environmental view of a failure of regulation to create and enforce effective open space requirements, but there is also a developer perspective on the difficulties of managing uncertainty in planning systems and the relative ease of repeating processes that have worked before, leading to the same results being repeated continuously [11, 14].

4.3 Regulation

4.3.1 Regulatory Controls and Other Influencing Measures

Studies considering the regulation applicable and contributing to this phenomenon have pointed in particular to the operation of setback requirements, site coverage percentages and landscaping provisions (including deep soil requirements). These regulatory mechanisms directly influence or control the area, shape and quality of private open space included in new residential developments.

There are also mechanisms that can indirectly influence private open space, in particular in the form of sustainability measures that include nature-based solutions, and water sensitive urban design (favouring permeable surfaces). These mechanisms are usually part of a building design code in state or territory legislation, or otherwise form part of local government building design requirements. Each of these mechanisms is discussed below.

4.3.2 Setbacks

Setback requirements are normally strict measurements setting the minimum distance allowed between the proposed building and the lot boundary. They apply to front, rear and side boundaries and they are usually small, around 1–2 m [3]. They can also differ for the upper storeys of buildings and be applied to restrict building height. For the most part setbacks are aimed at regulating issues surrounding privacy and aesthetic values, rather than environmental values. Larger setbacks for upper storeys are designed to allow daylight to reach the ground floor and to mitigate privacy concerns due to overlooking of neighbours. On larger land parcels, buildings may be restricted by way of a specified building envelope, rather than setbacks, in order to constrain built form to a particular area within the lot.

Although setback limits may have originally been intended to set a maximum building envelope within which to construct a building, it seems that landowners (and their architects or builders) often treat setbacks as a starting point for the outline of a building's footprint and shape. In Victoria, the setback provisions are so uniformly followed they have led to a recognisable residential building shape known as 'the ResCode barn':

> Of the many provisions of the Planning Scheme dictating urban form and building shape, ResCode's A10 and B17 (demonstrating building height and setbacks to side and rear boundaries) have been critical in setting a maximum development envelope that many architectural 'optimists' seek to realise to the full extent.
>
> …
>
> Regrettably, the formalisation of the envelope control as part of Clause 54 and 55 of the Planning Scheme (as opposed to a more fluid guide) has resulted in a void in creative thinking about how to deal with the critical profile of domestic buildings at the side and rear boundary interfaces [16, p 26]

With setbacks set at minimums for privacy and aesthetic concerns, and uniformly applied, the resulting private open space takes the form of 'residual' land: long, thin strips of land surrounding the dwelling [17]. These strips of land are usually unsuitable for supporting tree growth. Front setbacks are normally larger than side and rear setback requirements, but front setbacks are often planted with lawn rather than large trees and may have significant space taken up with wide driveways leading to double garages [3].

A study conducted of new developments on the urban fringe of Perth assessed whether the new developments met state government goals including access to the natural environment. Private open space was assessed as minimal, with many land parcels at less than 300 m^2 in total, some as low as 80 m^2. The predilection for large houses, together with state design code setbacks of 1.5 m, meant that much private open space generated was in the form of confined strips of residual open space. The author concluded that 'while outer suburban development delivered in Perth since 2004 can be seen to providing a connection to nature at a broader regional scale, at the lot scale this access to nature has been diminished' [10].

4.3.3 *Site Coverage Percentages*

Site coverage limits (sometimes called plot ratio) are often set, with 50% site coverage being a commonly cited percentage and Hall documenting a minimum of 40% ranging up to 70% in new suburbs [3]. By comparison, site coverage for older suburbs is generally less than 30% [3]. The current larger site coverage, in conjunction with the operation of setbacks, creates insufficient suitable open space for planting:

> Planning codes in different parts of Australia commonly stipulate that at most about half of a suburban lot can be covered by the dwelling. This might seem reasonable at first sight, but a 2 metre gap around the edge of the lot can easily occupy nearly half of the total area. Some codes require the provision of an outdoor area open to the sky, next to the main living area, but the minimum area is always very small, commonly 16 m^2 [17, p 15]

There is also a propensity to build square shaped or deep rectangular dwellings, perhaps because they tend to offer greater floor area for a lower building cost, which results in the shape of the rear garden being long and narrow, and therefore less useful for planting and for large trees [3]. In addition, site coverage limits do not always include semi-permanent structures, such as covered outdoor spaces or paved areas, which further reduce the available space for planting.

> The statistic that most clearly differentiates the form of newer Australian suburb from the older one is the larger proportion of the land area that is occupied by the dwellings. When taken together with patios, verandas and pergolas, and with the carriageways and driveways, the greater part – and, in some cases, nearly all – of the land area is tree-less and covered by impervious surfaces. Aside from the front lawns, only a small residue is permeable and planted [3, p 72]

4.3.4 *Landscaping and Deep Soil Areas*

Landscaping is provided for in the planning instruments of all Australian jurisdictions. This planning design requirement has been primarily aimed at ensuring aesthetic and amenity objectives are met. The introduction of deep soil or deep planting requirements, as part of site design, is more recently being included in planning policy instruments, including Western Australia, Victoria, South Australia and New South Wales. The deep soil requirements appear to have been initially included in high density development policies (medium to high apartment buildings) and are now beginning to emerge more widely in policy requirements for medium density developments.

The term 'deep soil' is usually defined by reference to a lack of structures: for example, in the *State Environmental Planning Policy (Housing) 2021 (NSW)*, 'deep soil zone' is defined as 'a landscaped area with no buildings or structures above or below the ground' [18]. Deep soil requirements are normally expressed as a percentage of the site area (this review has found examples that range from 5% to 50% of site area) together with a minimum dimension (examples range from 3 m to 6 m). By way of illustration, Table 4.1 describes the deep soil area requirements for apartment design in Victoria [19].

There is little academic literature on the use of deep soil zones in Australian urban planning, either explaining the dimensions or documenting the emergence of this design criterion. The case law is more prolific, revealing numerous disputes over the application of deep soil planning policies or design requirements, in particular in New South Wales. The disputes appear to focus on the correct percentage and dimension calculations [20], what may be included in the definition of deep soil zone [21], and whether meeting the applicable overall objective is more important than meeting precise calculated measurement requirements [22].

In WA, the residential design codes ('R Codes') for apartments were amended in 2019 to introduce a requirement for 'Tree canopy and deep soil areas', with 'deep soil area' defined as 'an area of soil that is free of built structure and has sufficient area and depth to support tree growth and infiltrate rainwater' [23]. This requirement provides that 10% of the site area should be deep soil area (or 7% if existing trees are retained) and specifies dimensions dependent on the size of the tree to be planted. It also provides that '[t]he location of deep soil areas should be determined early in

Table 4.1 Deep soil areas and canopy trees required for apartment design in Victoria. From Victoria State Government (2017) Apartment Design Guidelines for Victoria [19]

Site area (m^2)	Deep soil areas	Minimum tree provision
750–1000	5% of site area (minimum dimension of 3 meters)	1 small tree (6–8meters) per 30 m^2 of deep soil
1001–15,000	7.5% of site area (minimum dimension of 3 meters)	1 medium tree (8–12 meters) per 50 m^2 of deep soil, or 1 large tree per 90 m^2 of deep soil
1501–2500	10% of site area (minimum dimension of 6 meters)	1 large tree (at least 12 meters) per 90 m^2 of deep soil, or 2 medium trees per 90 m^2 of deep soil
>2500	15% of site area (minimum dimension of 6 meters)	1 large tree (at least 12 meters) per 90 m^2 of deep soil, or 2 medium trees per 90 m^2 of deep soil

Note Where an existing canopy tree over 8 meters can be retained on a lot greater than 1000 m^2 without damage during the construction period, the minimum deep soil requirement is 7% of the site area the design process and arboricultural advice obtained to ensure the deep soil areas can sustain trees' [23].

The deep soil requirement was considered by the WA State Administrative Tribunal in the case of *Kemstone Investments Pty Ltd v City of Joondalup* [24]. The Tribunal considered whether there was compliance with, amongst other things, the deep soil area requirements under the R Codes. The Tribunal found that the requirements were not met, partly as a result of the applicant's deep soil area provision appearing to have been considered late in the process, leading to difficulties in meeting the required deep soil dimensions:

> Whilst it might be true that the area of DSA [Deep Soil Area] for a medium tree (36 m^2) under table 3.3b may be - in strict terms - 'met', the DSAs are not ideal. They are triangular, significant portions of them have a dimension of less than 3 metres and it is also the case that each of them relies on permeable paving at some level. While it is no doubt the case that the size and shape of DSAs needs to be approached flexibly, the DSAs in this instance appear to be something of a design afterthought.
>
> ...
>
> To my mind, the over-arching intent of O 3.3.3 of the R Codes is to ensure that adequate DSAs are provided to ensure that adequate provision is made to enable trees to flourish and be appropriately integrated into developments so to ensure that the aesthetic and environmental benefits offered by trees can be delivered.
>
> ...
>
> The day has long passed where landscaping concepts, in the context of the medium and high density proposals under the R Codes, can be dealt with as a design afterthought [24, paras 54, 58 and 125]

In a later case, also in WA, a proposed development included deep soil areas that overlapped, and were overhung by a first-floor canopy. In that circumstance the Tribunal dismissed the review application on the basis that the landscaping (including deep soil areas) did not achieve the objective of the R Codes, concluding that this was a 'fundamental failing' [25] and commenting in particular that 'the landscaping arrangements have not been properly, nor appropriately, integrated during the design concept phase' [25].

4.3.5 Sustainability Requirements

Sustainability in building design in Australia has been driven by climate action, predominantly in the form of energy reduction goals. These are manifested in building star ratings (introduced by the private sector but not normally applying to the residential housing sector other than voluntarily) [26] or requirements set by local government for development applications to comply with certain sustainability measures. The influence of these measures on trees and planting in private open space often depend on the integration and uptake of 'greening' solutions for reducing energy consumption and increasing carbon sequestration. There is also a drive to use greening solutions on private land for climate resilience goals such as mitigation of the urban heat island effect and managing floodwater impacts.

In Australia, some methods for increasing green space on private land are being introduced by local governments as part of sustainability measures for new developments. For example, some local governments have introduced lists of sustainability measures and specified that development applications must include a certain minimum number of measures from the list, which includes greening options [27]. The City of Melbourne has introduced a Green Factor tool that requires certain new developments to reach a minimum score on a green rating system [28, 29] (Fig. 4.1).

There is an important difference between urban greening solutions in the form of planting on built form (such as green roof or walls) and solutions that take the form of planting on site [30]. Although planting on built form can be a solution for energy efficiency and carbon sequestration goals, it is regarded as generally difficult for built form to support sufficient deep soil for trees, especially large trees, or contribute to stormwater management solutions. These solutions require access to natural ground.

The use of urban greening solutions on built form means that a completed development, particularly a tall building, could have green space comprising more than 100% of the site area. For example, in Brisbane, a residential development application has been made for an apartment tower featuring planted sustainability measures with a green plot ratio equating to 200% of the site area, comprising 12% of site area as deep planting in natural ground and 188% of site area as containerised planting. Interestingly, the development application is being supported by the local government despite exceeding development height policies, which the developer states is the only way to make the development economically viable, and an exemption is being sought from the state government to allow the development to proceed [31].

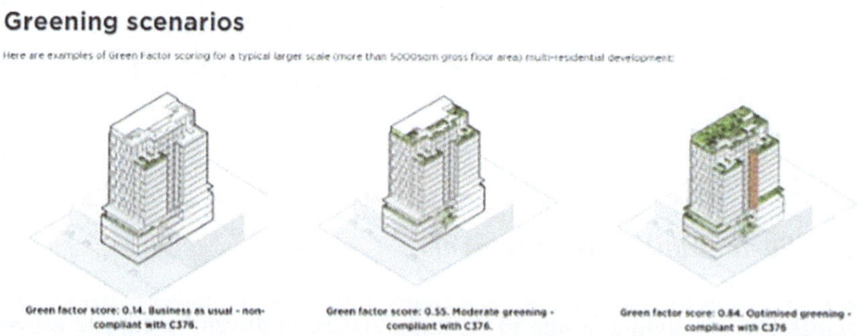

Fig. 4.1 Greening scenarios illustrating green factor scoring for a multi-residential development in Melbourne, Victoria. From City of Melbourne (2024) Green Factor tool [28]

4.4 Enforcement and Compliance

Few studies have examined enforcement of planning site regulation mechanisms relevant to urban green space. However, one recent study involved an ambitious audit of development applications against planning code and policy aims for provision and retention of private green space in urban consolidation. The study was conducted across a ten-year period for an LGA in Brisbane. Despite obvious frustrations with planning framework processes making the research task 'fraught and inaccurate', the authors concluded:

> Nonetheless, the findings indicated that DAs [Development Applications] submitted by developers and approved by Council were not consistent with the stated policy intent. While the Council's planning vision recognises the importance of urban trees and greenspace, non-compliant residential DAs and approvals in Taringa were submitted and approved despite not reflecting policy objectives.
>
> …
>
> In summary, the results of this research indicate that while the City Plan recognises the importance of residential greenspace, DAs approvals in Taringa did not reflect this vision, resulting in a significant decrease in private greenspace preservation and provision [32, pp 233 and 236]

Enforcement issues may be exacerbated by accelerated or alternative approval processes. In particular, where there is an ability for developers to bypass local government processes and seek approval from a state planning body, this can defeat local government capacity to ensure consistent enforcement of urban greening policies [32]. Similarly, when enforcement occurs through the court systems, rights of appeal are also constrained in the context of planning, particularly in WA where there are no third party rights of appeal [33]. Improved third party appeal rights could result in greater public participation and better decision-making [34].

There are also potential issues relating to compliance. Once a development application is approved, the resulting building may still differ from the approved application. This occurred in a case in NSW where the development application description complied with deep soil provisions, but as built, the development did not comply with those provisions. The Court noted that 'the failure of the applicant to construct the development strictly in accordance with the approved plans and conditions of consent has caused a large degree of contention' and confirmed that the local government was justified in seeking to have the development carried out properly [22].

4.5 Suggested Responses

Many suggested responses to the shrinking private garden focus on tighter planning restrictions, particularly setbacks and site coverage. Hall [3] recommended two simple changes to planning policies should be introduced:

- Minimum rear setback space of 8 m–10 m; and

- Limit building footprint to 35% of the land area.

In Hall's view, these changes would, together, be more than sufficient to change the physical form of Australia's suburban private open space. Hall also argued for active promotion of sustainable house and garden design (particularly with infill development).

Similar suggestions were echoed in a recent study from the perspective of improving biodiversity in Australian cities, where the authors suggested decreasing building footprint size, compensated for by increasing allowable storeys (the authors provide an example of 33% footprint with allowance for 3 storey dwellings), as well as the inclusion of deep soil zones [35].

In a recent study on Australian urban precinct regeneration, Newton et al. suggested:

- for small lot subdivision, planning mechanisms enforced by local government are critical to ensure that each small lot decision works towards the incremental improvement of urban nature; and
- for precinct scale developments, site layouts should be arranged to maximise onsite green infrastructure, including deep soil zones and setbacks, and buildings should be designed to integrate urban greenery in, on and over built form [36].

From the perspective of reducing energy consumption in buildings, researchers are also advocating the construction of smaller homes, as house size can have significant direct and indirect effects in determining energy consumption patterns. Acknowledging that direct regulation of measures such as setbacks and plot ratio may be politically challenging, alternative mechanisms are being suggested to reduce house size, such as taxation, financing models and support for innovative housing provision [37].

4.6 Conclusion

There is general consensus in the literature that a shift from urban fringe development to urban consolidation is a necessary step for advancing urban environmental and social outcomes. However, such a shift increases demand for urban infill, exacerbating the problems that result in reduced garden space and necessitating increased height in residential apartment buildings to accommodate population growth.

There is a general sense underlying most suggested responses that planning and other requirements designed to address reducing private green space are mandatory and not voluntary. As noted by Thomson et al. in relation to urban nature-positive design:

> Currently, no city can claim to be nature-positive although the concept is theoretically possible, and as outlined above, there are growing examples of how to design nature-positive solutions into urban environments. However, these opportunities may not be taken up unless the planning system encourages them. If such principles were not voluntary, as in rating

> systems such as Living Building Challenge, but rather were adopted as planning policy to systematically increase urban nature, this would allow urban development to be reframed from a degenerative, to regenerative force for urban nature [35, p 18]

In Australian cities, whichever measures are taken, it is perhaps most important that *something* is done to change the current trajectory: wherever there is urban renewal and new developments without a greening vision there are missed opportunities to bring relief [38].

References

1. Daniel C, Morrison TH, Phinn S (2016) The governance of private residential land in cities and spatial effects on tree cover. Environ Sci Policy 62:79–89. https://doi.org/10.1016/j.envsci.2016.01.015
2. Marshall AJ, Grose MJ, Williams NSG (2019) From little things: More than a third of public green space is road verge. Urban For Urban Green 44:126423. https://doi.org/10.1016/j.ufug.2019.126423
3. Hall T (2010) The life and death of the Australian backyard. CSIRO Publishing, Collingwood
4. Duckworth-Smith A (2015) Backyard bonanza: Improving the quality of 'popular' suburban infill. Australian Planner 52:297–313. https://doi.org/10.1080/07293682.2015.1086808
5. Australian Bureau of Statistics (2022) Land and housing supply indicators. https://www.abs.gov.au/statistics/industry/building-and-construction/land-and-housing-supply-indicators/2022
6. Stephan A, Crawford R (2016) Size does matter: Australia's addiction to big houses is blowing the energy budget. The Conversation
7. Newton P, Pears A, Whiteman J, Astle R (2012) The energy and carbon footprints of urban housing and transport: Current trends and future prospects. In: Tomlinson R (ed) Australia's unintended cities: the impact of housing on urban development. CSIRO Publishing, Melbourne, pp 153–189
8. Australian Bureau of Statistics (2024) Building activity, Australia. Data downloads, Building Activity Average Floor Area. In: Australian Bureau of Statistics. https://www.abs.gov.au/statistics/industry/building-and-construction/building-activity-australia
9. Vasek L (2009) A land where dwelling size and social status count. The Australian
10. Bolleter JA (2017) Fringe benefits? A review of outer suburban development on Perth's fringes in relation to state government goals concerning the natural environment and efficient transport connectivity. Australian Planner 54:93–114. https://doi.org/10.1080/07293682.2017.1319395
11. Goodman R, Buxton M, Chhetri P, et al (2010) Planning and the characteristics of housing supply in Melbourne [AHURI Final Report No. 157]
12. Foye C (2017) The relationship between size of living space and subjective well-being. J Happiness Stud 18:427–461. https://doi.org/10.1007/s10902-016-9732-2
13. Ribeiro C (2024) Homes on steroids: How Australia came to build some of the biggest houses on Earth. The Guardian
14. Kelly JF, Weidmann B, Walsh M (2011) The Housing We'd Choose. Grattan Institute, Melbourne
15. Dovey K, Woodcock I, Pike L (2015) Intensifying Melbourne: Transit-oriented urban design for resilient urban futures. Planning News 41:10–11
16. Czarny C (2008) Design in (the Planning World): Redefining the ResCode Barn? Planning News 34:26
17. Hall T (2015) What has happened to the Australian backyard? Australian Garden History 27:12–15

18. NSW Government (2021) State Environmental Planning Policy (Housing) 2021
19. Victoria State Government (2017) Apartment Design Guidelines for Victoria. https://www.planning.vic.gov.au/__data/assets/pdf_file/0030/80994/Apartment-Design-Guidelines-for-Victoria_August-2017.pdf
20. Frasers Lorne Pty Ltd v Goldsworthy Burke [2008] NSWLEC 743
21. Sixjay Newport Pty Ltd v Northern Beaches Council [2023] NSWLEC 1109
22. Mirvac Projects Pty Ltd v Ku-Ring-Gai Council [2007] NSWLEC 540
23. Government of Western Australia (2019) State Planning Policy 7.3 Residential Design Codes, Volume 2—Apartments
24. Kemstone Investments Pty Ltd v City of Joondalup [2020] WASAT 115
25. Bradshaw v City of Joondalup [2020] WASAT 156
26. Martek I, Edwards DJ, Seaton S, Jones D (2022) An appraisal of Australia's approach to promoting urban sustainability. Built Environment Project and Asset Management 12:262–276. https://doi.org/10.1108/BEPAM-07-2020-0130
27. City of Subiaco (2023) Innovative sustainability policy gets green light. City of Subiaco
28. City of Melbourne (2024) Green Factor tool. In: https://participate.melbourne.vic.gov.au/amendment-c376/green-factor-tool
29. Bush J, Ashley G, Foster B, Hall G (2021) Integrating green infrastructure into urban planning: developing Melbourne's green factor tool. Urban Plan 6:20–31. https://doi.org/10.17645/up.v6i1.3515
30. Pearlmutter D, Theochari D, Nehls T et al (2020) Enhancing the circular economy with nature-based solutions in the built urban environment: Green building materials, systems and sites. Blue-Green Systems 2:46–72. https://doi.org/10.2166/bgs.2019.928
31. Brisbane Development (2023) Green dreams renewed: Aria's taller 'urban forest' tower makes a comeback. https://brisbanedevelopment.com
32. Osborne LP, Cushing DF, Washington TL (2020) Changing greenspace in residential developments in an inner suburb of Brisbane, Australia. Australian Planner 56:228–240. https://doi.org/10.1080/07293682.2020.1824198
33. Willey S (2021) Planning and environmental law in Western Australia. Lawbook Co., Sydney, NSW
34. Willey S (2006) Planning appeals: are third party rights legitimate? The case study of Victoria, Australia. Urban Policy Res 24:369–389. https://doi.org/10.1080/08111140600877032
35. Thomson G, Newman P, Hes D et al (2022) Nature-positive design and development: A case study on regenerating black cockatoo habitat in urban developments in Perth, Australia. Urban Sci 6:47. https://doi.org/10.3390/urbansci6030047
36. Newton PW, Newman PWG, Glackin S, Thomson G (2022) Climate resilience and regeneration: How precincts can adapt to and mitigate climate change. Greening the Greyfields. Palgrave Macmillan, Singapore, pp 105–120
37. Clune S, Morrissey J, Moore T (2012) Size matters: House size and thermal efficiency as policy strategies to reduce net emissions of new developments. Energy Policy 48:657–667. https://doi.org/10.1016/j.enpol.2012.05.072
38. Jim CY (2013) Sustainable urban greening strategies for compact cities in developing and developed economies. Urban Ecosyst 16:741–761. https://doi.org/10.1007/s11252-012-0268-x

Chapter 5
Mandatory Tree Planting

Abstract Tree planting requirements on private urban land usually form part of development approval. These are often included as a condition of permission to remove a regulated tree or as part of the approved landscaping of a new development. Tree planting may also be mandated through sustainability requirements in developments, where tree planting is one of several listed sustainability options. Tree planting conditions normally specify the location and size of the new tree, and may include species selection and a provision to replant the tree if it dies. Energy efficiency is the main site-scale policy driver for tree planting requirements. Drivers at the neighbourhood-scale include urban heat island mitigation and biodiversity support. Water efficiency is often a factor at the regional scale. The larger scale drivers are usually considered in urban forest strategies for public land, but are not often part of the required considerations for mandatory private urban tree planting. Nevertheless, courts are tending to enforce developer consideration of tree planting early in the site design process, due to its significance for all of these reasons. Key problems with mandatory tree planting are tree morbidity rates and developer non-compliance.

5.1 Introduction

Mandatory tree planting requirements on private urban land usually form part of development approvals. These are often included as a condition of permission to remove a regulated tree or as part of the approved landscaping of a new development. Tree planting conditions may also be imposed as a sanction for unauthorised removal of a regulated tree (see Chap. 2), or a tree protected by a conservation covenant (see Chap. 3).

Tree planting conditions are normally set out in state/territory or local government planning instruments and may specify a range of detailed requirements, including:

- the number of trees to be planted
- the location of the trees
- the size of the trees at maturity (often noted as small, medium or large)
- species that are not to be planted (weedy species)

E. J. Scaife, *Urban Tree Protection on Private Land*,
SpringerBriefs in Law, https://doi.org/10.1007/978-981-95-1857-9_5

- the size of the tree at the time of planting, specified by pot/container size (in litres) or by stem height
- the area of soil surrounding the tree
- the proximity of existing or proposed built structures above and below ground.

Sometimes a general type of tree is also specified, for example shade trees may be required where planting is in a carpark, or indigenous trees may be required in landscaping or replacement planting. Occasionally a list of acceptable species is provided.

5.2 Problems with Mandatory Tree Planting

5.2.1 Replacing Significant Trees

The value of requiring new planting to replace a significant tree has been questioned. In a case involving an application to remove a significant tree under ACT laws (as they were at the time), the presiding Tribunal member commented:

> In recognition that removal of the tree would have some impact on streetscape and amenity, [it was] proposed that these concerns might be addressed by a condition on approval requiring the planting of a new tree, of greater floral or faunal significance, elsewhere on the block. However I consider that such a condition would be meaningless. First, it is unlikely that any new tree would be of greater floral or faunal significance than the present tree, given its age and size, and the known value of this species in attracting bird-life. Second, any tree that might be planted in compliance with such a condition could be removed by a subsequent lessee without sanction, provided that it did not reach a size that would qualify it as a "significant" tree [1, para 73]

The first-mentioned reason (unattainable significance) is reinforced by research into the impact of climate change on tree growth, with studies suggesting that, in future, many existing tree species will no longer have climatically suitable habitat to support growth and health in urban areas [2, 3]. Increasing the maximum standing life and the number of regenerating seedlings of large, old trees in urban areas have been identified as key factors in perpetuating the number of these trees over the long term [4].

The Tribunal member's second concern (that a young tree could simply be removed) may be addressed by including a condition requiring the planted tree to be replaced if it dies and (where blanket protections apply) that this replacement requirement continues to apply until the tree reaches sufficient measurement thresholds as to be protected. An alternative way of addressing this issue is to require security for the performance of tree planting obligations. For example, the Environmental Planning and Assessment Act (1979) (NSW) provides that:

> (3) Where a person is guilty of an offence involving the destruction of or damage to a tree or vegetation, the court dealing with the offence may, in addition to or in substitution for any pecuniary penalty imposed or liable to be imposed, direct that person—

(a) to plant new trees and vegetation and maintain those trees and vegetation to a mature growth, and
(b) to provide security for the performance of any obligation imposed under paragraph (a). [5, s 9.56(3)]

This can be achieved by a person entering into a deed with the local government. In relation to a tree damage offence, entering into such a deed may also be taken into account in the calculation of a penalty, as the planting is seen to mitigate the environmental harm [6, 7]. Interestingly, a court recently made a remediation order not only for planting new trees but also for weed removal and the installation of fauna habitat boxes [8].

5.2.2 *Monitoring and Compliance*

Beyond the assessment of a completed landscaping plan, monitoring of tree planting requirements is difficult and time consuming for local governments. In many cases, it is likely that monitoring is not carried out and compliance is simply assumed. In Toronto, a study exploring homeowners' replanting compliance found that 70% of all survey participants planted the required replacement trees, but where the replanting was associated with construction, the compliance rate dropped to 54%. The study found that enforcement of required replanting was minimal, and city staff had indicated that fines were rarely issued [9].

Where monitoring and enforcement are minimal, compliance rates may be more strongly influenced by landowner motivations for tree planting. A USA study investigating the motivations of landowners in choosing to accept or decline the offer of a free tree and planting service found that the main reasons for declining a free tree included not wanting any more trees than they had and landowner concerns about tree maintenance [10].

Where the problems with monitoring relate to difficulties with accessing private land, remote sensing technologies may be able to provide an alternative way of assessing changes in individual tree size and condition on private urban land [11].

5.2.3 *Tree Survival*

The first five years after a tree is planted is known as the establishment phase. According to a global review of tree mortality studies, for urban trees the median annual mortality rate for urban planted trees in the establishment phase was 6.6% to 7%. The review also noted a lack of studies relating specifically to private residential trees, but the few studies carried out showed annual mortality rates for private residential yard trees (across all ages) ranged from 3.8% to 6.6% with a median of

4.6%. By way of comparison, the annual mortality rates for natural forested trees were found to be 1%–3% or less [12].

The review also considered factors associated with tree mortality. Commonly cited biophysical factors associated with urban tree mortality are tree size or age, and species. Commonly cited human factors associated with urban tree mortality are stewardship, maintenance and vandalism (although this latter factor may be less significant in private residential gardens). Stewardship and maintenance were reported to have a positive impact on tree survival. Higher mortality rates were associated with unstable home ownership, lower income areas and lower property values.

Where landowners may carry out the planting without professional assistance, it is useful to consider whether planting techniques or skill are relevant to tree mortality. A research project linked to the Toronto replanting compliance study noted above [9] found the results suggested that trees planted by the landowners themselves have a higher mortality rate than when planted by contractors or specialist volunteers [13]. Similarly, planting techniques were mentioned in another case study in association with high rates of tree survival [12]. By contrast, a recent USA study looking at the reasons for the death of young urban trees (albeit planted on public land) found there was no significant impact on tree mortality based on who planted the tree [14].

The nursery production system for tree stock may also impact tree survival [14]. Australian Standard AS 2303:2018 *Tree Stock for Landscape Use* sets out standards for determining the quality of tree stock for landscape use, as an important first step in the development of a successful landscape tree. Some local governments specify that tree stock planted as a development condition must adhere to this standard. For a discussion of Australian Standards relevant to private urban trees, see Chap. 7.

5.2.4 Species Choices Made by Landowners

The future composition of the private urban forest is shaped by the past and current planting preferences and actions of residential landowners. Studies have shown that private urban trees tend to reflect limited species diversity [9] and a landowner preference for trees with denser, glossy-leafed foliage that typically require more water than other types of tree [15].

There is also a shift towards planting smaller trees. A 2013 study using size class analysis to deduce the dynamics of the private urban forest found clear evidence of this shift, and the authors commented on the implications of this shift:

> The finding that large trees are likely to be less common in private gardens than in the past is especially significant as large trees are widely regarded to deliver a disproportionate share of urban forest benefits (Moore 2009). For example, large trees tend to become independent of watering by humans as their roots gain access to groundwater, provide vital urban habitat for many native animal species, and may figure more prominently than small trees in social processes of placemaking (Wolf 2005), as they are highly visible in the landscape and are experienced as shared characteristics of a local place. Moreover, the challenging conditions and space constraints experienced by street trees mean that unless new and novel opportunities to plant large trees in public spaces (such as in the roadway) are afforded, the population

> of large trees will continue to decline. The canopy cover targets that are commonly used to indicate urban forest benefits by municipal tree managers will be considerably harder to deliver with a smaller private tree stock [15, p 79]

Many mandatory planting policies for new developments provide landowners with a choice of tree size that may be planted, nominated as small, medium or large, with fewer trees required the larger the tree species. Others specify that the tree size should be complementary to the proposed built form or be of a species that will reach a minimum specified height or canopy diameter by maturity.

Lower maintenance trees may also be an important factor to residents. A USA study of resident preferences indicated that greater resident support would be available for planting policies including smaller tree species and trees requiring less maintenance [16].

5.2.5 Ratio of Replacement Trees

Some local governments require replacement of removed trees to be at a higher ratio than 1:1. In *Albert Developments 3 Pty Ltd v Sutherland Shire Council*, the NSW Land and Environment Court confirmed tree planting orders (by consent) that were based on local government provisions requiring a tree replacement ratio of 8:1. As the applicant had two trees approved for removal, sixteen replacement trees were required to be planted [17].

This type of provision may, however, lead to irrational results. In *Tseng v Brisbane City Council*, the Queensland Court of Appeal considered an application for leave to appeal based on a tree removal contravention notice issued by the council. The notice applied strict ratio calculations to the unlawful removal of 62 trees, resulting in a requirement for the applicant to plant either 823 native trees and shrubs of tube stock size or 549 trees and shrubs of 45 litre stock size on her 1.5 hectare land parcel. The Court dismissed the application, but commented on the number of trees to be replanted:

> There may perhaps have been room for the applicant to challenge the contravention notice on administrative law grounds. The number of trees required to be replanted seems extraordinarily high given the area of the applicant's land; such a dense planting may have rendered the land unusable. OS21 does not expressly deal with calculation of replanting when there has been a contravention. More broadly it, and the calculation of the monetary amount, appear to be Council policies which were arguably applied by Council without any consideration as to whether or not they produced a rational or just outcome in the circumstances of the applicant's contravention and land. However, the applicant never advanced an administrative law challenge to the contravention notice, and there was no material before this Court which allows us to do more than speculate about these matters [18, para 14]

5.3 Emerging Opportunities for Advancing Urban Forest Aims

5.3.1 Incorporating Urban Forest Aims Across Private Land

Amenity value has been (and remains) a primary consideration reflected in landowners' and developers' residential plant and location choices [19]. Amenity, land value improvement, air filtration, storm water filtration and carbon sequestration are some of the more important goals associated with a general increase in the urban forest. Of increasing significance are other matters such as biodiversity support, cooling, reduced water usage, energy efficiency, environmental justice and accelerating canopy increase. The location and species of a tree are critical factors in achieving these urban forest aims.

On private land, requiring specific planting in accordance with these aims is difficult:

> While managers have a growing range of regulatory instruments at their disposal, the mandated planting of certain types of trees on private land is politically difficult to advocate and virtually impossible to implement [15, p 80]

Nevertheless, at the point of applying conditions for development approval or tree removal approval, there are opportunities for local governments or planning authorities to negotiate or impose specific planting in accordance with broader urban forest aims, especially those aims designed to benefit the wider community.

5.3.2 Energy Reduction

Localised or site-scale environmental benefits tend to focus on the role of trees in reducing energy consumption for heating and cooling. Studies in Australia and globally have demonstrated that the placement and species of tree on private land can make a significant difference to the energy reduction capacity of buildings on site and nearby. In Australia, recent research has been undertaken to develop a model for determining optimal residential tree volume and distance in a residential setting, relating to the use of trees for energy reduction and cooling effects for the benefit of the immediate residence and neighbouring properties. This research identified a number of key factors, summarised below:

- The orientation of a tree relative to the building is important. In Australia, planting to the west and to some extent the north is best for energy use reduction. Planting to the east can also benefit neighbouring buildings situated to the east.
- The distance between a tree and the building is another factor, to optimise shading, as the most significant cooling factor.

- Windy climates need different considerations than those with heatwaves and lower wind speeds: tree placement can be designed to reduce air movement, or to increase it.
- The proposed height of the building relative to the tree is relevant, as shade can only be cast where the tree is higher than the building. This influences the selection of tree.
- The number or volume of trees planted is not an ever-increasing benefit. Studies show that energy reduction benefits plateau after a certain point.
- Use of deciduous trees allows sunlight heating in winter months and blocking/ shading in summer months [20].

Climate change effects over time are also likely to impact the optimal placement and species of tree for heating/cooling on a given site [21].

In further research to identify how such optimal arrangements could be incorporated into Australian planning frameworks applicable to private land, the authors described this as a 'major challenge' as residents are unwilling to give up privately utilised space, but also noted that optimal planting policies can provide greater benefit overall than a policy emphasis on simply retaining existing trees, commenting that such policies are generally lacking in Australian residential design codes and planting guidelines [22].

5.3.3 *Mitigating Urban Overheating*

At the neighbourhood scale, the role of trees in mitigating heatwaves and urban heat island effects is well documented. Heat mapping can show where these effects are most dominant in the landscape and requiring shade trees to be planted in those areas can help to reduce the temperatures. There are additional benefits in reducing human heat-related mortality. A study modelling the potential for increases in canopy cover to reduce heat-related mortality in Adelaide showed that improved health benefits were possible from increasing canopy coverage across all LGAs in the study. The authors found 'a clear and urgent need for close alignment of public health policy with urban planning and greening policies for a whole of city's benefit' [23, p 269].

Carparks on private land are a particular topic of focus for planning policies and research on this type of planting in Australia. Similarly, in the USA, local policies requiring new tree planting in carparks constitute one of the most common types of tree regulation [24, 25]. Some existing local government policies require new developments that include carparks to provide for shade trees to be planted in a minimum ratio to the number of parking spaces, typically ranging from 1:4 to 1:6. The use of porous surfaces is also sometimes a requirement in carparks, for both tree growth and to reduce stormwater runoff.

5.3.4 Creating Biodiversity Links

A further neighbourhood scale benefit is the use of specific native plants to create biodiversity landscape links between parks and reserves. Mapping technologies are being used to determine optimal biodiversity linkages across landscapes, including linkages at smaller, neighbourhood scales. Where these optimal linkages cover private land, specific species planting in those areas can help to create links useful for expanding the habitat and food sources available to local wildlife. At present, most of these plantings are the result of voluntary and educational efforts, rather than being the subject of mandatory planting requirements on private land.

5.3.5 Reducing Water Consumption

Planting tree species that require less water to establish and are drought tolerant is important in regions where water shortages are either common already, or will become more so as a predicted result of climate change. This tends to be encouraged at state or territory regional level (for example, by water authorities) and is typically not the subject of mandatory planting requirements, but may have associated incentives for landowners (for example rebates).

5.3.6 Environmental Justice

Many studies have confirmed that urban tree cover is correlated with socio-economic demographics and related factors. Income, education levels and land values tend to be lower in urban areas with fewer trees. In urban forest strategies, these areas may be prioritised for tree planting, including on private land. As public land in these urban areas may offer reduced planting opportunities [26], sometimes due to deeper social inequities such as the pre-existing location of parks [27], planting on private land could present a more viable option. There is also a need to consider the complex topic of green gentrification (whereby increased property values from canopy improvements can lead to displacement of lower income residents) and to manage this potential effect when planning tree planting for environmental justice aims.

5.3.7 Accelerating Canopy Cover Increase

Across many local government areas, increasing the extent of canopy cover over a certain timeframe is often a measurable goal. Some research has been carried out to identify ways of accelerating canopy cover increase. There are doubtless many factors that can accelerate canopy cover, but three of the most significant are planting larger tree stock, planting larger species of tree, and the timing of planting.

A UK study modelling canopy cover increases has found that canopy cover may be boosted by requiring mandatory planting of larger tree stock [28] which can be specified by pot or container size, or stem height or stem diameter. However, other studies point to growth rates of larger tree stock being slower overall than that of younger stock [29], and that larger tree stock face additional root grounding challenges leading to reduced resilience to storm events [30].

As noted above, selecting or requiring the planting of large tree species rather than medium or small species tends to result in a significant and exponentially greater canopy coverage at maturity. A 2025 study modelling canopy cover growth on public land in a new development area within Greater Melbourne found that prioritising planting trees with a larger canopy at maturity would increase canopy cover on public land by 5.1%–6.9% compared with a scenario based on the current planting selection and design approach [31]. Similarly, a small-scale study carried out by the City of Ryde in NSW demonstrated the significance of the contribution of large trees to canopy cover by modelling results for four different sizes of tree in one street, finding that the canopy cover produced by planting nine large trees was more than nine times greater than the canopy cover produced by planting twenty trees of the default tree size [32].

Requiring the planting of large trees also has disadvantages, as selecting from a reduced number of species can decrease the resilience of the urban forest and its capacity to provide a range of ecosystem functions [33]. Further, the loss of one tree (for example, from pests, disease or drought) will have a greater negative impact on canopy cover, and finding locations suitable for large trees can be challenging, particularly on private land. Requiring the planting of large trees on private land also goes against the identified trend of private landowners to plant smaller trees.

Another key factor in accelerating canopy cover is the time of planting. Modelling has confirmed that investment in tree planting that maximises planting in earlier years, rather than planting evenly or later over the same timeframe, leads to significant canopy increases over that timeframe [28].

5.3.8 Conflicts in Urban Forest Aims

There may be conflicts in the choices made to achieve the above aims and therefore a need to prioritise planting aims for particular sites. For example, a tree planted to maximise the energy efficiency of a building may well have different choices made in relation to species and location than a tree planted to support local biodiversity. In a 2006 study of the conflicts and synergies between amenity values and urban biodiversity conservation, the author concluded that hard decisions may be required if biodiversity is to enjoy planning priority over amenity [34]. There is also a balance to be struck between trees planted for cooling and trees selected to reduce water consumption, as trees typically require irrigation to support optimal transpiration for cooling [35].

A collaboration group led by Hort Innovation has developed Which Plant Where, a free online tool for making species decisions considering several key factors including the location in Australia, the type of urban space, climate change suitability over time, heat and drought tolerance, biodiversity contribution and shade contribution [36]. This tool is sometimes incorporated into urban forest planning by local government and can be applied to planting on both public and private land.

5.4 Conclusion

Although tree retention has many benefits, others argue that in the longer term, planting the right tree in the right location is equally important, if not more so. Further, where deep soil space on urban residential land is becoming 'squeezed', it becomes vital to ensure the optimal placement and species of tree [22]. Currently, regulated planting of trees on urban private land is minimal [22] and there may be scope for the use of existing or new mechanisms to further increase, improve and shape the future urban forest.

Planning for the urban forest is essential to inform decisions about optimal tree species and location. There are many factors to consider, and urban forest plans can require difficult decisions about priorities, timing and investment. The choice of tree and location, along with provision for appropriate deep soil, need to be up-front considerations in new developments and replacement of regulated trees—not included as an afterthought. An urban forest plan that covers private land can help to inform appropriate landscape planning and negotiations between planning authorities, landowners and developers.

With a strategic plan in place, development proposals and applications for tree removal can be seen as opportunities to improve the future urban forest on private land. More opportunities will be likely to arise where tree removal exemptions are part of an exercise of discretion on the part of the local planning authority, rather than the same factor being an exclusion or operating without a discretionary aspect.

The rising understanding and importance of urban forest benefits to the community, in particular for biodiversity support and climate change mitigation, presents a mismatch with existing limited mandated planting mechanisms on private land. It is therefore likely that new regulatory mechanisms for planting on private land will be needed to increase and shape the future urban forest, and to do so rapidly. However, any successful new regulation of tree planting on private land will need widespread and ongoing community support. Further research would be useful to develop new alternative regulatory mechanisms and to test the level of public support for new regulatory mechanisms for tree planting on private land. It would also be valuable to better understand the key reasons for residential landowner engagement in large scale tree planting and stewardship initiatives on private land in the urban environment in Australia.

References

1. Mossop v Conservator of Flora & Fauna [2003] ACTAAT 22
2. Burley H, Beaumont LJ, Ossola A et al (2019) Substantial declines in urban tree habitat predicted under climate change. Sci Total Environ 685:451–462. https://doi.org/10.1016/j.scitotenv.2019.05.287
3. Nitschke CR, Nichols S, Allen K et al (2017) The influence of climate and drought on urban tree growth in southeast Australia and the implications for future growth under climate change. Landsc Urban Plan 167:275–287. https://doi.org/10.1016/j.landurbplan.2017.06.012
4. Le Roux DS, Ikin K, Lindenmayer DB et al (2014) The future of large old trees in urban landscapes. PLoS ONE 9:e99403. https://doi.org/10.1371/journal.pone.0099403
5. NSW Government (1979) Environmental Planning and Assessment Act 1979 No 203 [NSW]
6. Hornsby Shire Council v Moit [2001] NSWLEC 50
7. Pittwater Council v Scahill [2009] NSWLEC 12
8. Hawkesbury City Council v Saed [2022] NSWLEC 34
9. Conway T, Khatib J, Tetreult J, Almas A (2022) A private tree by-law's contribution to maintaining a diverse urban forest: Exploring homeowners' replanting compliance and the role of construction activities in Toronto, Canada. Arboric Urban For 48:9–26. https://doi.org/10.48044/jauf.2022.002
10. Morgan M, Ries PD (2022) Planting free trees on private property: Understanding urban residents' motivations and hesitations. Urban For Urban Green 71:127557. https://doi.org/10.1016/j.ufug.2022.127557
11. Klobucar B, Sang N, Randrup TB (2021) Comparing ground and remotely sensed measurements of urban tree canopy in private residential property. Trees For People 5:100114. https://doi.org/10.1016/j.tfp.2021.100114
12. Hilbert D, Roman L, Koeser A, et al (2019) Urban tree mortality: A literature review. Arboric Urban For 45. https://doi.org/10.48044/jauf.2019.015
13. Tétreault J (2021) Evaluating the effectiveness of Toronto's private tree by-law in reaching the city's urban forestry goals. Master in Forest Conservation (MFC) Capstone Papers, University of Toronto
14. Wattenhofer DJ, Johnson GR (2021) Understanding why young urban trees die can improve future success. Urban For Urban Green 64:127247. https://doi.org/10.1016/j.ufug.2021.127247
15. Pearce L, Kirkpatrick J, Davison A (2013) Using size class distributions of species to deduce the dynamics of the private urban forest. Arboric Urban For 39. https://doi.org/10.48044/jauf.2013.011
16. Conway TM, Bang E (2014) Willing partners? Residential support for municipal urban forestry policies. Urban For Urban Green 13:234–243. https://doi.org/10.1016/j.ufug.2014.02.003
17. Albert Developments 3 Pty Ltd v Sutherland Shire Council [2022] NSWLEC 1532
18. Tseng v Brisbane City Council [2022] QCA 222
19. Conway TM (2016) Tending their urban forest: Residents' motivations for tree planting and removal. Urban For Urban Green 17:23–32. https://doi.org/10.1016/j.ufug.2016.03.008
20. Rouhollahi M, Whaley D, Byrne J, Boland J (2022) Potential residential tree arrangement to optimise dwelling energy efficiency. Energy Build 261:111962. https://doi.org/10.1016/j.enbuild.2022.111962
21. Lin BB, Meyers J, Barnett G (2016) The role of urban vegetation for climate adaptation in cities. In: The 17th National Street Tree Symposium 2016. CSIRO Land and Water, Sydney
22. Rouhollahi M, Behrend M, Boland J (2024) Optimising tree arrangement policy in Australian small-scale residential settings. Sustain Cities Soc 102:105232. https://doi.org/10.1016/j.scs.2024.105232
23. Carlos B-K, Veronica S, Scott H, Ehsan S (2022) The potential for urban canopy cover to reduce heat-related mortality in Adelaide. In: Aghamohammadi N, Santamouris M (eds) Urban overheating: heat mitigation and the impact on health. Springer Nature, Singapore, pp 249–273

24. Koeser AK, Hauer RJ, Downey EE et al (2021) Municipal response to state legislation limiting local oversight of private urban tree removal in Florida. Land Use Policy 105:105398. https://doi.org/10.1016/j.landusepol.2021.105398
25. Hauer RJ, Peterson WD (2016) Municipal tree care and management in the United States: A 2014 Urban & Community Forestry Census of Tree Activities. Special Publication 16-1. Stevens Point
26. Danford RS, Cheng C, Strohbach MW, et al (2014) What does it take to achieve equitable urban tree canopy distribution? A Boston case study. Cities Environ (CATE) 7
27. Garrison JD (2019) Seeing the park for the trees: New York's "Million Trees" campaign vs. the deep roots of environmental inequality. Environ Plan B Urban Anal City Sci 46:914–930. https://doi.org/10.1177/2399808317737071
28. Walters M, Sinnett D (2021) Achieving tree canopy cover targets: A case study of Bristol, UK. Urban For Urban Green 65:127296. https://doi.org/10.1016/j.ufug.2021.127296
29. Watson WT (2005) Influence of tree size on transplant establishment and growth. Horttechnology 15:118–122. https://doi.org/10.21273/HORTTECH.15.1.0118
30. Gilman E, Miesbauer J, Harchick C, Beeson R (2013) Impact of tree size and container volume at planting, mulch, and irrigation on Acer rubrum L. growth and anchorage. Arboric Urban For 39. https://doi.org/10.48044/jauf.2013.023
31. Torquato PR, Szota C, Hahs AK et al (2025) Insufficient space: prioritizing large tree species and planting designs still fail to meet urban forest canopy targets. Landsc Urban Plan 256:105287. https://doi.org/10.1016/j.landurbplan.2024.105287
32. Garden J, Vanderberg J, Hooper J, et al (2023) Report for City of Ryde: Urban forest strategy. City of Ryde, Australia
33. Peterson G, Allen CR, Holling CS (1998) Ecological resilience, biodiversity, and scale. Ecosystems 1:6–18. https://doi.org/10.1007/s100219900002
34. Kelly AH (2006) Securing urban amenity: Does it coincide with biodiversity conservation at the local government level? Australas J Environ Manag 13:243–253. https://doi.org/10.1080/14486563.2006.9725139
35. Broadbent AM, Coutts AM, Tapper NJ, Demuzere M (2018) The cooling effect of irrigation on urban microclimate during heatwave conditions. Urban Clim 23:309–329. https://doi.org/10.1016/j.uclim.2017.05.002
36. Macquarie University (2024) Which Plant Where. https://www.whichplantwhere.com.au/

Chapter 6
Changing Land Ownership from Private to Public

Abstract As part of advancing any urban forest strategy, it is worth considering whether public land might be increased by converting land from private to public. In urban areas, public land is initially designated at the time of creating a new subdivision, when part of the subdivided land is ceded to the Crown, free of cost, for use as public open space. Around Australia, the base contribution levels vary from 5% to 12.5% of the developable land area. Land values are often high and courts deal with many disputes over this contribution. Private urban land may also be purchased or compulsorily acquired for public purposes by governments or statutorily designated authorities. These mechanisms involve payment of a purchase price or compensation as well as various ongoing costs, and obtaining funding is often difficult. The emerging concept of environmental infrastructure offers potential as a way of improving the allocation, design and funding for the conversion of private land to public open space.

6.1 Introduction

Public land managed by local government is significantly easier for local governments to use in achieving urban forest strategies than private land. As part of advancing any urban forest strategy, it is therefore worth considering whether the volume of public land might be increased to support an increase in urban forest. This means converting land from private ownership to public ownership. In urban areas, this may be achieved by the land being ceded to the Crown as part of urban development, by the compulsory acquisition of land, or by the purchase of land by a government body in the same way as any other land purchase.

At the outset of this chapter, it is important to acknowledge the troubled historic background to land ownership in Australia. As a colonised country, all Australian land was claimed by the British Crown under the doctrine of 'terra nullius' (land belonging to no-one). Land was parcelled and land titles sold or given to private ownership or leasehold, or some lesser (usually temporary) access right. Aboriginal custodians of the land have since successfully contended that the doctrine of terra

E. J. Scaife, *Urban Tree Protection on Private Land*,
SpringerBriefs in Law, https://doi.org/10.1007/978-981-95-1857-9_6

nullius should be rejected as a legal basis for land ownership, and that, at least in some instances where the private or public access rights conferred did not give exclusive possession, they remain the traditional owners of the land. This traditional ownership has been recognised as a form of legally enforceable land right known as native title [1]. In urban areas, native title will almost always have been extinguished, for example by the grant of freehold title or some other inconsistent use. For this reason, native title is not raised as a relevant issue impacting the matters discussed in this chapter. Nevertheless, with this background in mind, it is sometimes jarring to consider the mechanisms by which the Crown may take back land from private ownership and the multitude of legal disputes that ensue from attempts to do so.

6.2 Public Open Space

6.2.1 Defining Public Open Space

Perhaps the most significant way in which private land is converted to public land that may be used for urban forest creation is the initial designation of land in urban subdivisions as 'public open space'. This term, often known by the acronym 'POS' or sometimes as simply 'Open Space', is difficult to define in any universal way, both across jurisdictions and across time.[1] However, the history of public open space in Australia provides some insight into its changing definition.

The Australian concept of public open space as a development contribution followed the British usage in urban planning, where it was applied to create areas of publicly accessible open space for recreation and amenity in the development of new suburbs. Public open space therefore originally focussed on sports grounds and parks. There is a general consensus in the literature that the uses for public open space have, over time, expanded well beyond this original focus. Definitions of public open space now tend to include uses for climate change mitigation and adaptation, for biodiversity support and entail an increased emphasis on passive recreation [2, 3]. The role of public open space in human physical and mental well-being has been a particular focus of recent research, accelerated by responses to the Covid-19 pandemic [4], and prompting linked research into the environmental social justice aspects of access to urban green space as a public health resource[5]. With private gardens reducing in size, public open space carries greater significance in fulfilling these urban community requirements that might otherwise be provided by private open spaces [6].

By way of an example of the current, broader concept of public open space, in 2022 the NSW government introduced a public open space strategy [3], with the following introductory webpage description:

[1] In this review, the term 'public open space' is used to cover both Public Open Space and Open Space, unless otherwise stated.

> Open space is the foundation of liveable communities. Public open space is infrastructure that is essential for communities and creating great places to live. It encompasses parks, natural areas and linkages, waterways and foreshores, informal parklands, sports grounds and courts, playspaces, historical sites, and recreation trails for walking and cycling. It is found in every part of NSW — from remote regional towns to new greenfield suburbs, and long-established urban centres. Well-connected open space plays a crucial ecological, economic, social and cultural role in our lives.
>
> ...
>
> People with access to public open space are healthier and happier than those without. For many people living without access to a backyard, the open spaces in our communities are vital to maintain physical and mental health. [7]

The concept of public open space appears to be both expanding and shifting, with a reducing emphasis on active recreation requiring sports grounds and other turfed areas. Water conservation is an increasingly important factor in moving away from unnecessary turfed areas of public open space [8, 9]. Multiple use areas of public open space are commonly mentioned in current literature. The relatively recent introduction of biodiversity conservation as one of the functions of public open space provides many opportunities for multiple use, by combining passive recreation with natural spaces designed or preserved for biodiversity support. However, it is unlikely that biodiversity conservation purposes can be fully realised by designation as public open space, because public access to conservation areas is often inconsistent with best practice conservation principles [9, 10].

Clearly, the current suite of objectives for public open space in Australia presents a very different picture to the original British recreational and amenity value objectives for which the concept was originally created [2, 6].

6.2.2 *Development Contributions to Public Open Space*

In Australia, the subdivision of private land (for example, to create a new residential suburb) is not allowed without planning permission. State or territory legislation sets out powers for planning authorities to permit subdivision and allows for conditions of approval to be imposed, including conditions requiring a portion of the land for public open space to be ceded to the Crown free of cost.

The 1962 landmark case of *Lloyd v Robinson* [11] involved a dispute about the validity of this power as set out in Western Australian State legislation. The case concerned a developer who wished to subdivide an area of land, and had been required, as a condition of approval, to cede a portion of the land to the Crown for public open space, free of cost. The developer, not wishing to cede any land free of cost, argued that the legislation permitting this condition was invalid and claimed that the condition amounted to a confiscation of land without compensation. The High Court upheld the validity of the planning law, concluding that there was no confiscation effect; rather, ‘the inescapable effect of the Act is that the landowner must decide for himself whether the right to subdivide will be bought too dearly at the price of complying with the conditions' [11].

The requirement for public open space to be ceded free of cost remains objectionable to many developers. Although no longer about the validity of the relevant legislative power, disputes over public open space contributions have continued unabated in courts and tribunals across Australia. One editor observed that 'attempts to avoid POS have almost reached the point of becoming a national sport' [12].

6.2.3 Calculating Public Open Space Contributions

The primary basis for calculation of public open space contributions is usually expressed (in state or territory legislation) as a percentage of the development site area. Where the area percentage calculation is applied, the base level ranges from 5% to 12.5% depending on the State or Territory. Public open space contributions generally apply to standard land area subdivisions, strata subdivisions and to subdivision within a single building. There are also applicable minimum subdivision levels ranging from 2 lots to 20 lots, depending on the state or territory, whereby smaller subdivisions are either excluded from the public open space contribution requirements or require payment in lieu of a land contribution.

The area percentage calculation is based on an historically accepted standard of open space required per capita of 7–10 acres per 1000 people (approximately 30 m^2 per person) with an assumed uniform population density of 30 people per hectare. This basis for calculating public open space contributions was adopted from British and American standards dating back to the early 1900s, apparently with very little intervening consideration having been given to the appropriateness of the application of these standards in Australia, other than conversion to the decimal system [13]. In WA, the original 1955 plan setting the public open space calculation refers to Perth's abundant private open space as an assumption underpinning the entire plan, and differentiating WA from standards applicable in other countries:

> The primary source of outdoor recreation is the individual private garden. Where land is abundant and of comparatively low value, the almost universal desire for a garden can be satisfied. A garden is the first outdoor playground for the young child, the rest-park on the doorstep, the meeting place for friends and neighbours, even the small sporting arena for tennis and other games not requiring much space. It is, therefore, one of the basic assumptions of the Plan that the present demand by many people for relatively large lots will continue, and that those who want large gardens will not be prevented by planning restrictions from having them.
>
> When the population of the Region is 1,000,000 the average overall Net Residential Density should give an approximate total area of 35,0000 acres of private gardens, or about 35 acres per 1,000 persons. This figure is considerably in excess of standards applying in other countries (for example in England, where large areas of new development at average net densities of up to 14 houses per acre result in a standard of about 6 acres of garden space per 1,000 persons). Because of this, standards for providing incidental open space and children's playgrounds originating in England are not applicable in Western Australia. [14, pp 90–91]

Theses 1955 assumptions about private garden space in Perth no longer apply, where (as is the case across Australia) urban garden space reduces as density increases.[2] The public open space contribution percentages have been the subject of debate for many years, with a particular focus on the lack of flexibility to adjust with higher population density. This lack of flexibility is inherent in the use of area percentages, since they are based on a uniform population density assumption. Others argue that the percentages are too low, given the increased objectives associated with public open space and decreasing private garden space [6, 15]. One study found that the existing public open space is rarely fulfilling the related health and well-being objectives, suggesting that there may be a minimum threshold for meeting such objectives that is not reached by the existing standard provisions [16]. An industry report forecasting public open space for metropolitan Melbourne found that municipal open space stood at 23.5 m^2 per capita in 2023 and, on the basis of public open space contributions averaging 6%, this would fall to 18 m^2 per capita by 2043 [17]. Whilst it may be assumed that developers prefer certainty in relation to all contributions [18], some developers have expressed a preference for negotiating and planning public open space with the local government on a case by case basis rather than having a flat percentage applied [19].

Most local governments have powers to create policies setting a bespoke public open space contribution requirement applicable in their area, which could be higher or lower than the relevant base level, or may use a different calculation method altogether. However, there are four key issues with applying a higher percentage using this approach:

- This type of policy would usually need to be approved by the state government and would be subject to complex planning procedures and restrictions prior to approval being granted;
- There are typically restrictions on how local governments may use land designated as public open space, which may rule out certain types of desirable conservation land use even if the land were able to be obtained;
- In urban infill or strata scenarios, increased percentages may not be feasible as a way of providing additional land due to the overall development site land area being too small; and
- Due to the requirement to cede the land free of cost, the economic impact of increased public open space contributions on may dissuade or slow down development, or result in the increased cost of new lots passed on to buyers [18].

The possibility of hampering housing supply is of concern to local governments as well as state governments. For example, the City of Darebin in Victoria commissioned research into an appropriate bespoke public open space contribution percentage, which resulted in a report finding 'strong justification' for a rate of 18.2% of site area based on a 30 m^2 per capita public open space requirement and taking into account the net land areas remaining available for subdivision. However, the authors of the report considered this rate would hamper development and moderated their

---

[2] See Chap. 4 for a detailed discussion of research findings on this topic.

recommendation to a rate of 10%, commenting that this was still double the rate applied in many other Melbourne municipalities [20].

To overcome the housing supply issues, and provide a larger area of public open space, there is evidence of a growing trend to find other ways to ensure the provision of additional land for public open space in greenfield subdivisions or large redevelopment areas. For example, the local government (or other authorised government body) may conserve, purchase or acquire land from the developer prior to, or as part of, the development process. This means the developer contributions remain at the same level, but the area of public open space is increased. In other words, it de-couples developer contributions of land from the overall provision of public open space in a development. The remaining problem is funding the additional land (where necessary), but this problem may be preferable as it is not seen as hampering development.

Increased public open space requirements (whether by developer contribution or by other means) would provide additional land in large urban developments that could be used for increasing the urban forest. By way of visual reference, the two plans below demonstrate examples of a structure plan showing approximately 10% public open space (including drainage areas) (Fig. 6.1) and, by contrast, a structure plan with approximately 30% public open space (including drainage, developer contribution and land conserved by other means) (Fig. 6.2).

6.2.4 Design of Public Open Space

The design of public open space is also significant when considering urban forest objectives, particularly for mitigating urban heat island impacts or creating cross-landscape biodiversity linkages [9]. State or territory legislation often sets out certain requirements for public open space design, typically based on metrics designed to increase human health and well-being [16]. For example, some states require minimum park sizes or that a certain percentage of residents live within a certain distance from a park. However, these 'catchment' metrics tend to create a fragmented design of public open space and, although research on outcomes is limited, many of these metrics do not appear to achieve their related health and well-being objectives [16]. Other objectives such as climate change adaptation and biodiversity corridors may be better served by different design metrics facilitating green linkages and nature-based solutions across the entire area [23].

Public open space design (and contribution levels) can also be determined using a case-by-case, needs-based approach. This type of approach takes into account factors such as the existing landscape features, recreational needs, climate change adaptation and biodiversity at an early stage in the structure planning process.[3] With a needs-based design approach, there are considerable complexities involved in assessing and

[3] For example, see the Sustainable Subdivisions Framework developed by the Council Alliance for a Sustainable Built Environment [27].

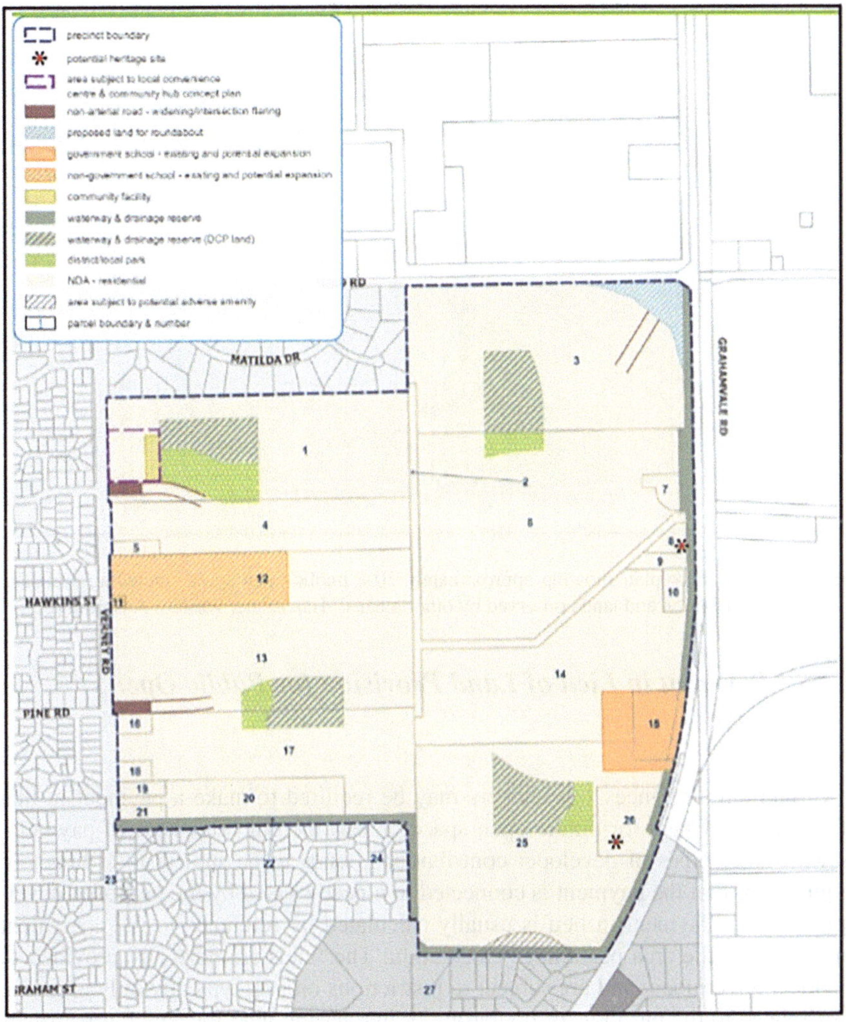

Figure 6.1 Structure plan showing approximately 10% public open space (including developer contribution and drainage). Shepparton, Victoria [21].

determining an appropriate public open space area and design for new subdivision developments or urban consolidation developments [24, 25]. Despite the complexities, needs-based approaches to both the area and design of public open space appear to be gaining favour with Australian local governments [26, 27].

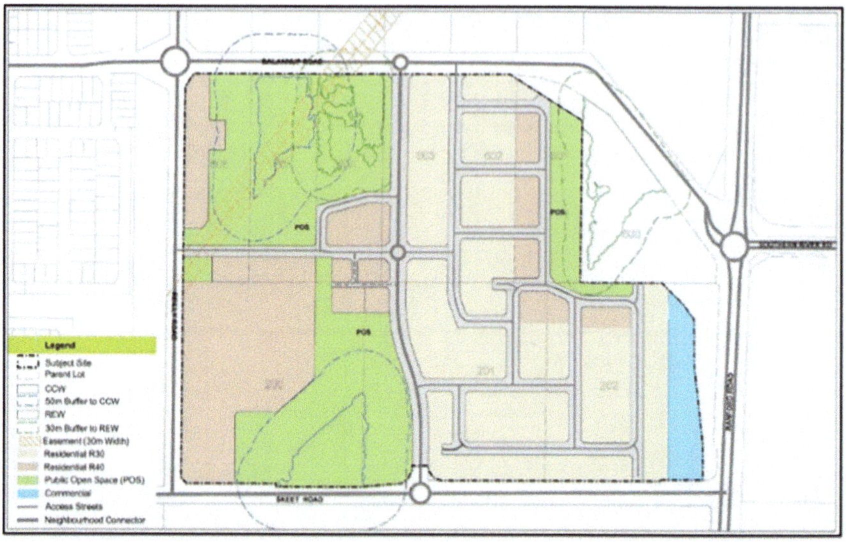

Figure 6.2 Structure plan showing approximately 30% public open space (including drainage, developer contribution and land conserved by other means). Harrisdale, Western Australia [22].

6.2.5 Payment in Lieu of Land Provision for Public Open Space

In certain circumstances,[4] developers may be required to make a payment in lieu of provision of land for public open space or part thereof. This type of payment, as with other types of developer contributions, tends to be subject to a threshold requirement that the payment is connected to a need caused by the proposed development [28]. Payment in lieu is usually calculated by reference to the equivalent land value of the area percentage calculation. The funds are normally provided to the local government and are subject to restrictions on use, typically only allowing uses related to the purposes of upgrading or purchasing land for public open space in the local government area.

Litigation concerning public open space payment in lieu is commonplace.[5] In particular, payment in lieu has been disputed as being a form of unauthorised tax [28]. This argument was discussed in a 2009 VCAT decision, *Stubbs Street Kensington v Melbourne City Council*:

---

[4] Typically, payment in lieu occurs in infill developments, where the land area is relatively small. In these situations, the percentage calculations would lead to only a small land area being provided, either too small physically for any useful public open space purpose, or too small relative to the intended future population on the development site land area.

[5] Disputes concerning public open space payment in lieu relate to matters such as the applicable date of valuation, the way the land is to be valued for the purposes of assessment (for example, improved or unimproved, and with or without subdivision permission) and the timing of any payment due.

> In my view, there is no justification for attempting to demonise public open space requirements as some form of tax that, as a matter of principle, the Tribunal should seek to constrain. Public open space requirements are a long standing and recognised means by which councils can collect money to help pay for the acquisition and upgrading of public open space land and facilities for the benefit of the community. The objective is not to tax development, but to provide councils with a source of land or funds to help carry out a legitimate and beneficient responsibility. As communities evolve, it is incumbent on councils to maintain, improve, upgrade and add to public open space facilities as a means of meeting the social needs and changing demands for passive and active open space. Councils are encouraged to prepare public open space strategies and may include open space objectives and strategies in the local planning policy framework of their planning schemes [29, para 15]

From a local government perspective, the funds provided by these contributions may not cover the cost of acquiring land for public open space. For example, the City of Melbourne, in its submission to the Victorian *Inquiry into environmental infrastructure for growing populations*, stated:

> Our current public open space contribution scheme, whether it be land or cash that developers are required to contribute, does not meet the needs for the range of open space that we have seen to offset the amount of development that is happening in the City of Melbourne. When I say a 'range of open space' needs, we are talking about active recreation needs, passive recreation needs, and water-sensitive urban design within landscapes. Essentially the property prices within Melbourne outstrip the cash we receive in terms of acquiring new land for public open space [30, pp 116–117]

There is evidence of some movement towards differentiating the contribution rates for development in established areas from that in greenfield developments. The aim is to provide local governments with additional funding for the purchase of land in established urban areas, in recognition of the higher costs of doing so. In some jurisdictions the movement is towards higher percentages, lower minimum thresholds and including other types of development such as industrial and commercial. However, others point to the additional rates contributions that infill development creates, arguing that this should be sufficient to provide additional income stream for local governments to acquire or improve public open space.

6.2.6 Public Open Space and population growth

In theory, a proper application of public open space based on population or dwelling density would mean that, as urban densities increase, the loss of private green infrastructure is offset by increased public green infrastructure. A CSIRO study designed to test this theory reviewed Sydney's tree cover and dwelling density, and found that the opposite was true. With greater dwelling density there was a decrease in residential tree cover and the '[r]esults also indicated a small decrease in the area of parkland within a suburb with an increase in dwelling density … As such, we found that there is not a greater amount of public parkland in high density residential areas to offset lower amounts of private green cover' [31]. This theory was also discussed in research conducted for the Brisbane City Council, which noted the complexity of understanding the social and cultural requirements of open space in higher density residential areas [24].

In established urban areas, it can be challenging for local governments to locate, fund and maintain suitable land for additional public open space as density increases. At state and territory level, there is an emerging acknowledgement of these challenges and a consequent need for change in public open space legislation and policies [30]. For example, in 2023, the WA Department of Planning, Lands and Heritage produced a draft policy document on public open space contributions, based on retention of the existing contribution percentage method, but noting that future legislative reform may be necessary.

> [I]t is anticipated that future reforms to planning for POS will investigate other methods of calculating the contribution for POS – this may include a set fee per lot contribution to replace the current percentage mechanism for calculating contributions, as well as reviewing when POS contributions are made. The changes being considered as part of this stage will require legislative change for them to be able to be implemented. [32]

It is seen as increasingly important for local governments to have a strategy for public open space, particularly in areas of urban consolidation where population density is expected to increase [2, 3, 33]. *Open Space for Everyone*, a strategy prepared for metropolitan Melbourne, states: 'the social, environmental and economic challenges the city and its people face mean we cannot continue to plan for open space as we have in the past' [34].

6.3 Land Purchase for Green Space

Australian governments also have powers to purchase private land by agreement with a landowner. By purchasing private land, governments may be able to boost the area of Public Open Space and, subject to restrictions related to the funding source, use the land for purposes that would increase the urban forest within their local government area. This may include public open space, reserve creation or other conservation uses.

A case study example of a local government purchasing land for environmental protection was included in the Greener Spaces Better Places 2020 benchmarking report on canopy cover:

> In 2019, Logan City Council used Environmental Levy funds to purchase a 47 hectare parcel of land called Bahrs Scrub for conservation and regeneration. The purchase of this land contributes significantly to the council's green infrastructure network. Given the type of land within the City of Logan, there is a lot of emphasis on the preservation of wildlife and habitat corridors and Voluntary Conservation Covenants on land. [35, p 35]

When purchasing private land, governments are required to pay market value for the land in the same way as any other buyer. In urban areas, the market value of the land may reflect its speculative future development potential, which is typically much higher than the value of the land used as public open space [25, 30]. For this reason, local governments often view the purchase of land at full market value as prohibitive where the land will be used for public open space or conservation, rather than development. As recently identified by the Victorian *Inquiry into environmental infrastructure for growing populations* [30], this leads to a number of problems:

- Land purchase by local government is favoured in areas where the values are lower, which is normally situated away from the areas of growing development pressure, where new public open space is most needed;
- In a rising property market, the retention of funds by local government reduces the purchasing power of those funds over time; and
- The purchase of land between governments may be subject to a requirement that the land is valued according to its 'highest and best use'—leading to a higher value placed on the land that does not necessarily reflect its intended use for conservation or as public open space. This type of purchase requirement creates an inter-government high value transaction that reduces remaining local government cash reserves available for the purchase of private land.

When considering the purchase of private land for public open space, local governments also need to take into account the cost of any rehabilitation required (for example on a contaminated site), transformation of the land to its new use as public open space or conservation, and ongoing maintenance of the land.

Land purchase by government may be used in greenfield developments to supplement the developer public open space contribution. Advance planning for this type of land allocation has the advantage of allowing early identification and preservation of land areas with particular conservation value. It also allows the purchased land to be de-coupled from the rules relating to public open space, if necessary.[6] The Western Australian State Government's 'Bush Forever' program demonstrates the advantages of advance planning for conservation including areas of private land [36]. However, government plans to purchase or acquire pre-identified private land for conservation or open space may also stall, possibly due to funding constraints and issues such as failed negotiations with private landowners [30].

Where there is a long-term plan for open space including privately owned land, and funding is readily available, the gradual purchase of the private land in accordance with the plan can lead to considerable cost savings when compared to an approach that involves purchase of land (or compulsory acquisition) on an immediate-need basis. This was the subject of a report by the WA Planning Commission (WAPC) describing the advantages of the Metropolitan Regional Improvement Fund (MRIF), including a case study involving private land purchased for conservation:

> ...2100 ha of land required for the protection of groundwater and conservation at Lake Pinjar was progressively acquired between 1994 and 2006 using the MRIF for \$25.25 M; in the absence of the MRIF the alternatives of purchase by negotiation or compulsory acquisition would have cost \$102 M and \$120 M respectively. The WAPC report provides valuable

[6] Despite developer attempts to argue the contrary, reserves within a development area are generally considered additional to public open space developer contribution and thus do not allow a developer to reduce their required contribution.

evidence to support the contention that land can be confidently reserved for future acquisition (generally at the owner's timing) only when backed by a large secure fund at the disposal of the acquiring entity [37, p 208]

The land purchase mechanism for creation of public open space relies on a willing seller of private land as well as the availability of the required funds. If a landowner does not wish to sell their land, this mechanism cannot work and will need to be supplemented by compulsory acquisition (see below).

6.4 Compulsory Acquisition of Land for Green Space

All Australian governments, and some government authorities, have statutory powers of compulsory acquisition that can be used to require a landowner to relinquish their land for public purposes. Typically, there is also a requirement for the provision of compensation to the dispossessed landowner, but this is dependent on a statutory right to compensation, which is not always provided [38, 39].

When using this mechanism to increase the available public open space, a local government or statutory authority might acquire private land in a variety of different circumstances. In broad terms, these are: land with a special conservation value; land within a proposed large subdivision development needed to supplement the developer contribution; small land parcels within an established urban area to form smaller green spaces such as pocket parks; or as part of a strategy to assemble a group of landholdings for a precinct redevelopment.

However, using compulsory acquisition powers is far from straightforward [40]. Compulsory land acquisition is one of the most controversial aspects of planning law. Courts tend to interpret this power very narrowly, in accordance with the statutory presumption against an intention to interfere with private property rights [41]. This means it is difficult to be certain that an attempted use of this power will be held valid by a court, and disputes are costly and time-consuming to resolve. For example, in 2007, Parramatta City Council compulsorily acquired two properties as part of an assembly of land for a precinct redevelopment. These acquisitions were disputed and, after two years of court proceedings, the High Court of Australia held the acquisitions were invalid. It was found that the Council's planned re-sale of the properties to a developer was a use that constrained the acquisition power, even where the re-sale was part of a larger plan for redevelopment[7] [42]. In another example, a compulsory acquisition by the WA Planning Commission was found invalid by the High Court of Australia in *Mandurah Enterprises Pty Ltd v WA Planning Commission.* The High Court found that the land in question was not specifically reserved for a public purpose

[7] For further discussion of the use of compulsory acquisition powers for assembly of land for redevelopment, see Pocock's discussion in 'Orgies of Seizure and violence: Compulsory acquisition and private sector redevelopment – lessons for Australia'[63]; Sheehan and Ginka's chapter 'Compulsory acquisition of private property rights for densification in Australia' [64]; and the policy discussion by Gallagher et al. in 'Parcel amalgamation as a mechanism for achieving urban consolidation through densification: The fixity of property boundaries over time' [65].

(in that case, construction of a railway), nor did it amount to a purpose incidental to the railway construction, as the acquisition power was exercised in order to avoid an obligation to construct a level crossing for access to the otherwise inaccessible site [41].

In greenfield developments, the acquisition power may be the only option for providing additional public open space where the area of land for this purpose falls short of local government objectives and the local government is unable to reach agreement with a developer. In the South Australian case of *Scali v City of Playford*, this effect was noted by the court:

> While it is open to a Council to set out, in the Development Plan, the desired location of public open space in its area, the extent to which it is able to realize its open space objectives will be determined by the pattern of land division undertaken in its area and the manner in which the provisions of s 50 [of the Development Act 1993 (SA)] are invoked by individual land division proposals. Where, as is the case here, a land division proposal is of a kind requiring a financial contribution to the Planning and Development Fund, rather than provision of land for open space purposes, the Council's only recourse, short of reaching agreement with the applicant and the Development Assessment Commission for provision of land in lieu of a financial contribution pursuant to s 50(2)(d), is to use its compulsory acquisition powers. [43, para 23][8]

Where compulsory acquisition occurs, there is a requirement for payment of compensation to the dispossessed landowner. Compensation is a broader concept than market value, as it aims to put the dispossessed person into as similar a position as possible as if the dispossession had not happened. This means the amount of compensation may include not only the value of the acquired property but also other costs related to dispossession, such as stamp duty costs, re-location costs, legal fees, valuation fees, mortgage transfer fees, and may include non-financial disadvantages suffered such as spiritual and cultural losses. For example, the *Land Acquisition (Just Terms Compensation) Act 1991 No 22* (NSW) provides:

55 Relevant matters to be considered in determining amount of compensation

> In determining the amount of compensation to which a person is entitled, regard must be had to the following matters only (as assessed in accordance with this Division)—
>
> (a) the market value of the land on the date of its acquisition,
> (b) any special value of the land to the person on the date of its acquisition,
> (c) any loss attributable to severance,
> (d) any loss attributable to disturbance,
> (e) the disadvantage resulting from relocation,
> (f) any increase or decrease in the value of any other land of the person at the date of acquisition which adjoins or is severed from the acquired land by reason of the carrying

[8] The ultimate effect of this may be that a local government pays more for acquiring the land than the funds provided in lieu of land contribution, in respect of the same land. This factor may influence developers to avoid land contributions in kind. In the *Scali* case, a council representative observed that developers staged subdivisions into allotments of 20 or less so each subdivision would fall below the South Australian threshold for provision of Public Open Space in kind [43].

> out of, or the proposal to carry out, the public purpose for which the land was acquired. [44, s 55]

As with purchasing land, using compulsory acquisition powers can be costly and the expense can be difficult to justify where the market value of the land is higher than its value where the intended use is public open space.

Where private land is reserved through zoning or equivalent measures, or its future use curtailed by government intervention, there is typically no statutory obligation to provide compensation to the landowner, since it is not an acquisition. There may be statutory rights to compensation where the intervention impacts the land value, but this may not be possible to demonstrate until the landowner wishes to sell the land [45]. In these situations, there is a policy tension between private property rights and public spend that can be difficult to resolve. Early acquisition of reserved land is a partial solution that has been raised [46], and another suggestion is the imposition of a purpose-specific land tax as a way of providing the necessary funding to compensate landowners for land use restrictions [37]. As discussed above at 6.2.3 and 6.3, this mechanism can be useful in urban greenfield developments to supplement the developer contribution with reserved areas for public open space.

6.5 Environmental Infrastructure and Private Land

The concept of environmental infrastructure (often known as 'green infrastructure') is emerging in Australia as a concept likely to facilitate sustainability and human health and well-being goals in urban areas [30, 47, 48]. This topic is very broad, and literature on green infrastructure is rapidly expanding [49, 50], particularly in the US, the UK and Australia [49]. The following paragraphs focus only on those aspects of environmental infrastructure that may impact the conversion of private land to public land.

6.5.1 *Expansive Definition*

As noted above, the definition of public open space has expanded and shifted over time. It is now expected to cover environmental objectives well beyond its original scope and intention. Environmental infrastructure, by contrast, facilitates a potentially expansive definition that covers all of the contemporary environment related objectives that public open space—as a concept—struggles to encompass. A multitude of definitions have been proposed in the literature, with some authors commenting that there is no singe definition emerging [49]. Many of the broader definitions are similar to that proposed by Benedict and McMahon, in their book *Green Infrastructure: Linking Landscapes and Communities*, as 'an interconnected network of natural areas and other open spaces that conserves natural ecosystem values and functions, sustains clean air and water, and provides a wide array of benefits to people and wildlife' [51]. Using a broadly defined concept would allow a definitional step change and facilitate a more fitting approach to encompassing all of the objectives associated with green space in urban areas.

6.5.2 Integrated Design

Where the design of public open space has typically focussed on human health and recreation goals, the concept of environmental infrastructure emphasises a holistic approach to urban design, taking into account all of the related objectives, ideally working together as an integrated system. Greenfields plans may achieve a wider range of green space design objectives by taking an environmental infrastructure approach to design, rather than a typical recreation-based approach discussed above. However, the wider range of objectives can also lead to complex decisions and potential trade-offs between various objectives [52].

6.5.3 Elevated Status

Introducing the concept of 'infrastructure' elevates the importance of environmental objectives as a necessary component of urban planning, included alongside other long-standing types of important public infrastructure. This was one of the themes emerging from the Victorian government's *Inquiry into environmental infrastructure for growing populations*. For example, the following comment was made in a submission to the inquiry by Dr Meredith Dobbie, Chair, Victorian Environment Committee, Australian Institute of Landscape Architects:

> We encourage an ecosystems management approach to urban planning and design, and landscape management. We believe that environmental infrastructure and green infrastructure need to be formally positioned in state policies and strategies, explicitly with ideally ecosystems services targets, which can then be evaluated and responded to post-occupancy assessment to see if in fact these targets are being reached, and if not, why not, and then future development can be improved as a consequence. We would need explicit environmental infrastructure, green infrastructure legislation, presumably through the planning scheme. [30, p 54]

6.5.4 Integration with Other Infrastructure

Perceiving environmental infrastructure as equivalent to other types of infrastructure encourages opportunities for cost-effective integration of different types of infrastructure. This can provide useful synergies, for example, stormwater drainage requirements designed using Water Sensitive Urban Design methods, road reserves designed to incorporate green infrastructure elements[9] and minimise impervious surfaces, or buildings designed with green infrastructure as part of the built form. In particular, the use of green infrastructure to reform stormwater drainage is gaining attention [53].

> Dr Bruce Lindsay, Senior Lawyer, Environmental Justice Australia, spoke about stormwater management at a public hearing, outlining that reforming stormwater management is key to facilitating improvements in urban environments. This is due to urban stormwater systems essentially inverting natural hydrology and ecosystem dynamics: after rain events, water drains rapidly into streams, the volume and timing of which can degrade and pollute water, instead of rain slowly entering streams and replenishing vegetation. [30, p 227]

This type of reform may have a potentially significant application to private urban land. In the US, some cities have introduced a land tax based on the proportion of impervious surface area on private land, integrating stormwater drainage with green infrastructure using regulatory measures producing both cost savings and public income. However, a primary focus on hydrology may lead to its prioritisation over other functions and benefits of green infrastructure [52, 54].

6.5.5 Valuation

Valuation of environmental infrastructure is a burgeoning topic of economic and accounting literature [55]. There appears to be a particular focus on valuing the cost savings produced by the health benefits and energy use reductions that green infrastructure provides [55, 56]. Other key areas include valuation of ecosystem services; measuring the cost savings from using green infrastructure instead of built or 'grey' infrastructure to achieve a particular objective, such as stormwater drainage; and measuring property values as a way of determining landowners' implicit willingness to pay for different levels of green infrastructure (hedonic pricing) [57]. Sometimes methods are combined to deliver an overall valuation for investment in green infrastructure [55, 58].

Valuation provides important input into decision-making on policies, priorities and funding. For example, Tapsuwan et al. [59] carried out a benefit-cost analysis of Canberra's green infrastructure to assist with decision making concerning Canberra's canopy target of 30%:

> In this analysis, we applied a stochastic whole-of-life benefit–cost analysis following the System of Environmental-Economic Accounting (SEEA) framework to compare alternative long-term management strategies for living infrastructure in Canberra, Australia. Spatially explicit data, i-Tree Eco and benefit transfer methods were used to estimate the stocks and flows ecosystem services benefits of urban forests and irrigated open spaces from 2018 to 2070. Our analysis suggests that a '30 per cent canopy cover expansion' scenario has the

[9] Research conducted for the Victorian Planning Authority suggested, amongst other things, that subdivision planning of road reserves 'let down' tree canopy potential by failing to provide sufficient space for medium to large canopy trees [66].

highest benefit–cost ratio, while the business as usual scenario, where a net loss of 400 trees is expected per year, offers the lowest benefit–cost ratio. [59, p 37]

It has been suggested that a system of payment for urban ecosystem services could provide funding to support future urban ecosystem management [60]. See Chap. 7 for further information on valuation.

6.6 Conclusion

It is possible that the existing concept of public open space is reaching the end of its useful life. Originating from a desire to provide a suitable amount of recreational public space to urban residents with large private gardens, over the past two decades it has been called upon to satisfy an ever-expanding range of green space objectives. However, the metrics built over time to support the provision of public open space (such as the space each person requires for recreation, or the walking distance to a park) do not easily lend themselves to the expanded range of objectives—in particular the task of ameliorating the urban impacts of global crises.

Where land is reserved for special conservation values in advance of any urban development, it creates additional green space, but this is can still lead to a fragmented landscape depending on the landscape design. Where land is not endowed with any special conservation values, the high costs typically associated with funding the purchase or acquisition of additional land are a significant barrier to the provision of suitable additional public open space. Ongoing maintenance also presents a funding issue.

The emerging concept of environmental or green infrastructure presents a potential way forward in developing a new way of perceiving, allocating, designing and investing in public open space that is more aligned with the current suite of objectives. This could include converting private land to public land in greater amounts and in different ways, such as the integration of environmental infrastructure with other types of infrastructure.

The entanglement of developer contributions with the amount of public open space provided in developments is a recurrent problem. Conflating these concepts produces an often-litigated tension between housing supply and the provision of green space that is clearly unhelpful in the short term, and in the longer term can create intractable problems. Avoiding this conflation may assist developer contributions to public open space to be considered separately from the myriad objectives that environmental infrastructure is called upon to deliver. This type of change could facilitate greater alignment between developers' goals and the amount and design of environmental infrastructure, as well as greater co-ordination in the design of different types of infrastructure. It may also highlight the need for other stable funding sources to fill any gap between developer contributions and the cost of the land area required.

These potential changes require further considered research and extensive public discussion to explore and test the viability of new regulatory mechanisms for creating public open space from private land. In Victoria, this has already begun, with the 2022 *Inquiry into environmental infrastructure for growing populations* [30]. International case studies indicate there are many challenges ahead [61] and that funding for securing compliance with any new regulatory mechanisms remains one of the key barriers to increasing public open space [62].

References

1. Mabo v Queensland (No 2) (1992) 175 CLR 1
2. Inspiring Place Pty Ltd, HM Leisure Planning Pty Ltd (2010) Tasmanian open space policy and planning framework—Main Report
3. NSW Government (2022) Public Open Space strategy for NSW: A coordinated long-term plan
4. Bolleter J, Edwards N, Cameron R et al (2022) Implications of the Covid-19 pandemic: Canvassing opinion from planning professionals. Plan Pract Res 37:13–34. https://doi.org/10.1080/02697459.2021.1905991
5. Astell-Burt T, Feng X, Mavoa S et al (2014) Do low-income neighbourhoods have the least green space? A cross-sectional study of Australia's most populous cities. BMC Public Health 14:292. https://doi.org/10.1186/1471-2458-14-292
6. Grose MJ (2009) Changing relationships in public open space and private open space in suburbs in south-western Australia. Landsc Urban Plan 92:53–63. https://doi.org/10.1016/j.landurbplan.2009.02.006
7. NSW Government Planning: Open Space. https://www.planning.nsw.gov.au/policy-and-legislation/open-space. https://www.planning.nsw.gov.au/policy-and-legislation/open-space. Accessed 6 Jun 2024
8. Doll CA, Burton MP, Pannell DJ, Rollins CL (2022) How green is green enough? Landscape preferences and water use in urban parks. Working Paper, School of Agricultural and Resource Economics, University of Western Australia 35 pp. https://doi.org/10.22004/ag.econ.320820
9. Grose M (2012) Considering ecological imperatives in public open space in a global hotspot of biodiversity. Landsc Rev 13:6–25
10. Kelly AH (2005) Facilitating picnics and nature rambles: conserving nature for recreation on local government open space—a viable option? Local Gov Law J 11:109
11. Lloyd v Robinson (1962) 107 CLR 142
12. Planning Institute of Australia (2009) VCAT decisions: public open space requirements—more uncertain territory. Plan News 35:24–27
13. Veal AJ (2013) Open space planning standards in Australia: In search of origins. Australian Planner 50:224–232. https://doi.org/10.1080/07293682.2012.739567
14. Stephenson G, Hepburn JA (1955) Plan for the metropolitan region, Perth and Fremantle, Western Australia, 1955: A report prepared for the Government of Western Australia
15. Grose MJ (2007) Perth's Stephenson-Hepburn plan of 1955: 10% POS, and housing then and now. Aust Plan 44:20–21. https://doi.org/10.1080/07293682.2007.9982608
16. Hooper P, Boruff B, Beesley B et al (2018) Testing spatial measures of public open space planning standards with walking and physical activity health outcomes: Findings from the Australian national liveability study. Landsc Urban Plan 171:57–67. https://doi.org/10.1016/j.landurbplan.2017.12.001
17. Spiller M, Noesgaard J (2024) Public open space contributions in Victoria: A preferred approach
18. Ruming K, Gurran N, Randolph B (2011) Housing affordability and development contributions: new perspectives from industry and local government in New South Wales, Victoria and Queensland. Urban Policy Res 29:257–274. https://doi.org/10.1080/08111146.2011.592136
19. Urban Development Institute of Australia—SA Division (2020) Developers want to revamp the rules of Open Space. https://www.udiasa.com.au/developers-want-to-revamp-the-rules-of-open-space/

20. SGS Economics & Planning Pty Ltd (2019) Open Space Contributions Review
21. Greater Shepparton, Victorian Planning Authority, Victoria State Government (2019) Shepparton North East precinct structure plan. Greater Shepparton
22. Hex Design & Planning (2022) Structure Plan Harrisdale North. City of Armadale, Western Australia
23. Şenik B, Uzun O (2022) A process approach to the open green space system planning. Landsc Ecol Eng 18:203–219. https://doi.org/10.1007/s11355-021-00492-5
24. Byrne J, Sipe N, Searle G (2010) Green around the gills? The challenge of density for urban greenspace planning in SEQ. Aust Plan 47:162–177. https://doi.org/10.1080/07293682.2010.508204
25. Maruani T, Amit-Cohen I (2007) Open space planning models: A review of approaches and methods. Landsc Urban Plan 81:1–13. https://doi.org/10.1016/j.landurbplan.2007.01.003
26. Byrne J, Sipe N (2010) Green and open space planning for urban consolidation—a review of the literature and best practice
27. Council Alliance for a Sustainable Built Environment (2023) Sustainable Subdivisions. casbe.org.au. https://www.casbe.org.au/what-we-do/sustainable-subdivisions/. Accessed 22 Jun 2024
28. Nolan D, Christie N (1999) Financial contributions as a market mechanism and the Resource Management Act 1991. N Z J Environ Law 3:127
29. Stubbs Street Kensington Pty Ltd v Melbourne City Council [2009] VCAT 1947
30. Legislative Assembly Environment and Planning Committee (2022) Inquiry into environmental infrastructure for growing populations. Parliament of Victoria
31. Lin BB, Meyers J, Barnett G (2016) The role of urban vegetation for climate adaptation in cities. In: The 17th National Street Tree Symposium 2016. CSIRO Land and Water, Sydney
32. WA Department of Planning, Lands and Heritage (2023) Draft operational policy 2.3 planning for public open space. https://www.wa.gov.au/government/publications/draft-operational-policy-23-planning-public-open-space
33. Planning Institute of Australia (2022) Connected with PUBLIC OPEN SPACE (Western Australia)
34. Victoria State Government (2021) Open space for everyone: Open space strategy for metropolitan Melbourne 2021. Melbourne
35. Hurley J, Amati M, Deilami K, et al (2020) Where will all the trees be? The 2020 update of green cover benchmarking in our cities and suburbs. https://www.greenerspacesbetterplaces.com.au/media/163303/wwattb_v13.pdf. Accessed 14 Dec 2023
36. Government of Western Australia (2022) Bush forever policy. https://www.wa.gov.au/government/publications/bush-forever-policy
37. Foley N, Williams P (2016) Funding and governance of regional public land acquisition in Perth and Sydney. Urban Policy Res 34:199–211. https://doi.org/10.1080/08111146.2015.1059321
38. Sheehan J, Brown J (2019) The compensation catapult. Pac Rim Prop Res J 25:21–38. https://doi.org/10.1080/14445921.2019.1598008
39. The Commonwealth v New South Wales (The Wheat Acquisition Case) (1915) 20 CLR 54
40. Raff MJ (2002) Planning law and compulsory acquisition in Australia. In: Callies DL, Kotaka T (eds) Taking land: Compulsory purchase and regulation in Asian-Pacific countries. University of Hawaii Press, Honolulu
41. Mandurah Enterprises Pty Ltd v Western Australian Planning Commission (2010) 240 CLR 409
42. R & R Fazzolari Pty Ltd v Parramatta City Council (2009) 237 CLR 603
43. Scali v City of Playford [2006] SAERDC 55
44. NSW Government (1991) Land Acquisition (Just Terms Compensation) Act 1991
45. Houweling T (2001) Compensation for reserve land under the WA metropolitan Region Town Planning Scheme Act. National Environmental Law Review 4:
46. Government of Western Australia (2021) State planning policy 3.6 infrastructure contributions. Western Australia

47. Lin BB, Meyers JA, Barnett GB (2019) Establishing priorities for urban green infrastructure research in Australia. Urban Policy Res 37:30–44. https://doi.org/10.1080/08111146.2018.1523054
48. Pakzad P, Osmond P, Corkery L (2017) Developing key sustainability indicators for assessing green infrastructure performance. Procedia Eng 180:146–156. https://doi.org/10.1016/j.proeng.2017.04.174
49. Parker J, Zingoni de Baro ME (2019) Green infrastructure in the urban environment: A systematic quantitative review. Sustainability 11:3182
50. Ying J, Zhang X, Zhang Y, Bilan S (2022) Green infrastructure: Systematic literature review. Econ Res-Ekonomska istraživanja 35:343–366
51. Benedict MA, McMahon ET (2012) Green infrastructure: Linking landscapes and communities. Island Press
52. Meerow S (2020) The politics of multifunctional green infrastructure planning in New York City. Cities 100:102621. https://doi.org/10.1016/j.cities.2020.102621
53. Webber JL, Fletcher TD, Cunningham L et al (2020) Is green infrastructure a viable strategy for managing urban surface water flooding? Urban Water J 17:598–608. https://doi.org/10.1080/1573062X.2019.1700286
54. Grabowski ZJ, McPhearson T, Matsler AM et al (2022) What is green infrastructure? A study of definitions in US city planning. Front Ecol Environ 20:152–160. https://doi.org/10.1002/fee.2445
55. Symons J, Jones R, Young C, Rasmussen B (2015) Assessing the economic value of green infrastructure: Literature review. Climate Change Working Paper No 23. Melbourne
56. Bowen KJ, Parry M (2015) The evidence base for linkages between green infrastructure, public health and economic benefit. Paper prepared for the project Assessing the Economic Value of Green Infrastructure
57. Rossetti J (2013) Valuation of Australia's Green Infrastructure: Hedonic Pricing Model using the Enhanced Vegetation Index. Monash University
58. Mekala GD, Jones RN, MacDonald DH (2015) Valuing the benefits of creek rehabilitation: Building a business case for public investments in urban green infrastructure. Environ Manage 55:1354–1365. https://doi.org/10.1007/s00267-015-0471-7
59. Tapsuwan S, Marcos-Martinez R, Schandl H, Yu Z (2021) Valuing ecosystem services of urban forests and open spaces: application of the SEEA framework in Australia*. Aust J Agric Resour Econ 65:37–65. https://doi.org/10.1111/1467-8489.12416
60. Richards DR, Thompson BS (2019) Urban ecosystems: A new frontier for payments for ecosystem services. People Nat 1:249–261. https://doi.org/10.1002/pan3.20
61. Zuniga-Teran AA, Staddon C, de Vito L et al (2020) Challenges of mainstreaming green infrastructure in built environment professions. J Environ Plan Manag 63:710–732. https://doi.org/10.1080/09640568.2019.1605890
62. Boulton C, Dedekorkut-Howes A (2024) How funding scarcity and ineffective governance tools inhibit urban greenspace provision: An exploration of municipal greenspace managers' insights. Landsc Urban Plan 251:105172. https://doi.org/10.1016/j.landurbplan.2024.105172
63. Pocock M (2015) Orgies of seizure and violence: Compulsory acquisition and private sector redevelopment—lessons for Australia. LGLJ 20:27
64. Sheehan J, Glinka C (2018) Compulsory acquisition of private property rights for densification in Australia. In: Searle G (ed) Compulsory property acquisition for urban densification, 1st ed. CRC Press LLC, pp 166–172

65. Gallagher R, Liu Y, Sigler T (2019) Parcel amalgamation as a mechanism for achieving urban consolidation through densification: The fixity of property boundaries over time. Land Use Policy 89:104239. https://doi.org/10.1016/j.landusepol.2019.104239
66. Hip v. Hype Sustainability, for the Victorian Planning Authority (2021) Barriers and solutions for increased tree canopy in Victoria's new communities. https://vpa-web.s3.amazonaws.com/wp-content/uploads/2022/03/Precinct-Structure-Planning-Guidelines-Barriers-and-Solutions-for-Increased-Tree-Canopy-in-Victorias-New-Communities-HIP-V.-HYPE-November-2021.pdf. Accessed 5 Jul 2024

Chapter 7
Standards and Valuation

Abstract Australian Standards are voluntary standards that can be incorporated into legislation or agreements. Three of these standards are relevant to private urban trees: AS 2303:2018 Tree Stock for Landscape Use; AS 4373-2007 Pruning of Amenity Trees; and AS 4970-2009 Protection of Trees on Development Sites. These three standards are widely used by local governments to specify nursery stock to be used in planting as a development condition; pruning that may be done without a permit, and tree protection conditions during construction, respectively. Tree valuation methods are not the subject of an Australian Standard, although one was drafted and re-drafted several times before being abandoned. In the context of private urban trees, monetary valuation is often undertaken to determine fines for tree damage offences, tree bond amounts, or to calculate compensation or damages for trees removed or damaged. Formulaic valuation methods commonly used in Australia include the Revised Burnley Method and the Thyer Method. Different valuation methods produce differing results for the same tree. Market valuation of urban trees derived from property values has shown that trees on private land have lower values than trees on public land, possibly resulting from landowners bearing the costs of private trees.

7.1 Introduction

Some authors have suggested there is evidence that trees can, in theory, live indefinitely: that they do not always have a natural aging and death process; rather they are subjected to external events that cause their eventual decline and death [1]. This, albeit provocative, idea underscores the importance of creating and maintaining suitable conditions for trees to thrive, for as long as possible. Various ways in which trees may be supported to live long and healthy lives are documented by the Australian Standards for tree stock, pruning and protection of trees during construction. These three standards are used in many contexts to promote health and longevity in trees.

Valuation of trees is not the subject of an Australian Standard (and may never be). The valuation of urban trees is complex and much depends on the specific context of the valuation and the particular characteristics of the subject tree. One particular

E. J. Scaife, *Urban Tree Protection on Private Land*,
SpringerBriefs in Law, https://doi.org/10.1007/978-981-95-1857-9_7

aspect of valuation relates to the lifespan of a tree, as some valuations have built-in assumptions that a tree's lifespan should be the same as a human lifespan. However, this assumption is disputed by others:

> I here re-state my argument against using human life-span as this horizon: trees are societal assets, and offer benefits to other humans beyond the life-span of one particular human; does a tree cease to have value, because the people alive in its later life are not here to witness it at present? I believe not. [2, p 218]

If best practice can be applied in the care of urban trees, it may be possible to extend their lifespan and, it follows, increase their value, by extending their health and longevity beyond one human lifespan.

7.2 Tree Stock Quality

Australian Standard AS 2303:2018 *Tree Stock for Landscape Use* (**AS 2303:2018**) refers to measurable and observable criteria that can be used to determine the quality and health of tree stock. Some local governments specify that tree stock planted as a development condition must adhere to this standard. This is reflected in several judgements of the NSW Land and Environment Court where conditions of development are often set out in full. In addition to specifying the quality of the tree stock (by reference to AS 2303:2018), other matters relevant to early tree survival may also be described in the conditions. For example, a condition applied to a recent development alteration approved by the Court included the following:

> Any replacement or supplementary tree shall be grown in accordance with Tree stock for landscape use (AS 2303:2018) and shall be a minimum container size of 100L at the time of planting. The replacement tree shall be planted in *deep soil landscaped area* and maintained in a healthy and vigorous condition. If the replacement tree is found to be faulty, damaged, dying or dead before it attains a size whereby it becomes a prescribed tree in accordance with Chapter E.3 of Council's Development Control Plan, it must be replaced with another of the same species which is consistent with the Landscape Plan…
>
> The project arborist shall document compliance with the above condition. [3, Annexure A, para E25]

For further discussion on tree survival and other matters relevant to mandatory tree planting conditions, see Chap. 5, above.

7.3 Tree Protection on Development Sites

7.3.1 Australian Standard AS 4970-2009 Protection of Trees on Development Sites

According to Cooper [4], '[i]t is the practice of some builders to "accidentally" run over the roots of trees that they would prefer to remove, but have not been granted permission' [4]. Even without malicious intent, a failure to properly protect trees during construction can result in the unintended death of a tree: trees adjacent to construction activities are more likely to die than trees not exposed to construction activities [5]. Studies have shown that tree protection measures reduce the rate of decline of trees during construction [6–8].

In Australia, is it common for local governments to stipulate tree protection conditions as part of any development approval that involves retaining trees on or adjacent to the site. Often these conditions will refer to the Australian Standard 4970-2009 *Protection of Trees on Development Sites* (AS 4970-2009). AS 4970-2009 was developed to document best practice measures for the protection of trees during construction. Based on a similar British Standard, AS 4970-2009 focuses on three key requirements: a qualified arborist, a tree protection zone and a root protection zone.

7.3.1.1 Project Arborist

A suitably qualified project arborist is required to be involved for the duration of the project. Sign off and certification from the arborist is required at the conclusion of the project, including a phase for rectification. There is some evidence that the involvement of a project arborist is significant in the successful retention of healthy trees during construction [7].

7.3.1.2 Tree Protection Zone

Establishing a tree protection zone is the primary means of tree protection specified in AS 4970-2009. The tree protection zone is an area surrounding the tree with a minimum radius of 2m, and otherwise with a radius generally calculated according to the size of tree, based on a formula of diameter at breast height (DBH) × 12.[1] The tree protection zone requires protective fences and signage, and is subject to restricted activities. AS 4970-2009 also includes a raft of alternative measures designed to protect a tree where incursions into the tree protection zone cannot be avoided.

[1] Based on US studies of tree stress, some authors have suggested that a minimum factor of 15 would be more effective for tree protection [65, 66].

7.3.1.3 Root Protection

According to AS 4970-2009, root damage is the most common form of tree damage associated with construction. AS 4970-2009 has a particular focus on ensuring the tree's root zone (and in particular the structural root zone)[2] remains protected. Root damage impacts may not be apparent until after the construction phase, as trees may take many years to decline and eventually die from root damage.[3] For this reason, monitoring is critical to ensure compliance during building works. In AS 4970-2009 monitoring is included in the project arborist role.

7.3.2 Tree Bonds

Tree protection during development may be reinforced by the imposition of a tree bond, involving the payment of money as security for the performance of the obligation to protect a regulated tree. Tree bonds appear to be used routinely in some jurisdictions in relation to trees on public land, to ensure the protection of public trees that may be impacted by private development. It is less common to use tree bonds in relation to trees on private land [9], however this usage may be increasing. For example, tree bonds, including for trees on private land, were recently introduced in the ACT under the Urban Forest Act (2023) (ACT) [10].

The amount of a tree bond will normally depend on a valuation calculation prescribed by regulation or policy. In the ACT, the minimum tree bond is $3000 [11]. In the case law, specified tree bond amounts range between approximately $1000–$115,000 [12, 13], but the higher figures often cover multiple trees.

There are few studies on tree bonds or their efficacy. Tree bonds were noted in a study exploring tree protection mechanisms around the world, but the authors only found one instance of tree bonds applying to trees on private land [9]. In the case law, tree bonds are not mentioned in any jurisdiction other than NSW.[4,5] A small number of the NSW cases relate to trees on private land. Two of these cases are noteworthy, for different reasons.

The case of *Hunters Hill Council v Gary Johnston* [14] concerned four protected trees on private property that were the subject of a tree bond of $20,000 (covering the four trees, at $5000 per tree). Despite having paid the tree bond and carried

[2] Despite common belief that the root zone of a tree matches its crown, studies show that the root zone normally extends well beyond the crown of a tree [67]. The structural root zone (as defined in AS 4970-2009) is a much smaller area immediately surrounding the trunk.

[3] This may be partly as a result of root damage pre-disposing a tree to decline from other co-occurring causes [68].

[4] It is possible that, in other jurisdictions, landscaping bonds cover the protection of existing trees to some extent.

[5] The cases appear to predominantly refer to tree bonds as a non-controversial condition of development approved by the court or tribunal. Most cases also appear to relate to tree bonds to protect public street trees adjacent to development activities, rather than protected trees on private land.

out the required tree protections, once development was completed the landowner deliberately removed the trees, possibly in order to reveal views from his newly constructed residence. The court ordered that the tree bond be forfeited and imposed an additional fine of $40,000.

The second case of significance is *Mirvac Projects Ltd v Ku-ring-gai Council* [15]. In that case, the developer disputed a number of development approval conditions, including a tree bond of $100,000 imposed by the council to protect significant trees on the property. The court considered that, where the replacement cost for each tree was $3500, the bond amount was such that the underlying motive was imposition of a penalty.[6] The court considered it more appropriate to impose a tree replacement condition, so protected trees would be replaced and nurtured until they would come under the council's tree preservation order.

7.4 Pruning of Urban Trees

7.4.1 Background

Pruning of trees originated in fruit and timber production, as a means of improving yield. Other types of trees, those located in developed areas and not typically associated with production, are known as 'amenity trees' or sometimes 'ornamental' or 'landscape' trees [16]. In urban areas, pruning of amenity trees is particularly important because it is seen as a way to enable the growth of trees in close proximity to buildings and people:

> With urbanisation a growing concern, trees are more precious to us than ever before and more trees must be planted amongst us in order to maintain a balanced dynamic system. Trees have never been more under threat. Knowing how and when to prune can allow us to coexist in harmony. Trees were never viewed as importantly as they are today and we should give them appropriate treatment so that they continue to thrive and provide their inestimable benefits to us and the whole environment. We owe them this much. [17, p 224]

A major change in understanding the impacts of pruning on trees came about in the 1980s, resulting from the use of the newly available handheld chainsaw to vertically dissect trees and discover the damage caused by prevailing pruning methods. In documenting these practices, the author, Alex Shigo, observed that '[p]runing improperly done is the worst injury that can be found on trees worldwide' [18]. Shigo's work prompted a general shift in thinking towards pruning practices that worked with trees' defence mechanisms to aid their recovery after pruning. Revised pruning practices began to be introduced and documented in a number of countries, to encourage best practice in pruning methods [17, 19].

---

[6] The court applied the Newbury test [69] (principles to determine if a planning condition is validly imposed) in making this finding.

7.4.2 Australian Standard AS 4373-2007 Pruning of Amenity Trees

In Australia, the first standard on pruning of amenity trees was published in 1996. It was updated and superseded in 2007 by the current version, AS 4373-2007 *Pruning of amenity trees* (AS 4373-2007). Amenity trees are defined in the standard as trees with recreational, environmental, aesthetic and similar values, and excludes trees for production purposes. AS 4373-2007 specifies methods for pruning of trees and provides guidance on correct and uniform practices intended for use on amenity trees. It includes an initial requirement to assess the tree for health and vigour, but the bulk of the standard addresses best practice for branch cutting and similar applied practices. AS 4373-2007 is focussed on the safety and health of the tree, so that the tree is not adversely affected by pruning. It does not address wildlife habitat or the safety of the tree worker.

In relation to tree protection mechanisms, AS 4373-2007 is sometimes used where trees are protected, but pruning is permissible. For example, AS 4373-2007 may be incorporated in conditions attached to development approval where trees are required to be protected during construction works, or in local government policies as part of allowable pruning practices that are exempt or excluded from tree damaging activities. These uses are usually stated in conjunction with a limitation on pruning severity.

7.4.3 Pruning Severity

Pruning severity refers to the percentage of canopy removal, sometimes referred to as foliage or total leaf area. Pruning severity is often referred to in local government laws to define acceptable pruning, as compared to excessive pruning that would be considered a tree damaging activity and thus require approval.

In Australian legislation, pruning severity differs between jurisdictions. For example, ACT legislation limits allowable pruning to 10% of canopy per year [10] and in South Australia, the limit is up to 30% of the tree crown every five years [20]. Limits may be somewhat arbitrary as they appear to have no clear scientific basis. AS 4373-2007 is silent on appropriate pruning severity, referring only to safe canopy removal percentages as being species and age specific. The literature on pruning severity relates predominantly to production trees, and suggests that there is a wide range of pruning severity (20%–80%) that can be undertaken without impacting long term tree growth, depending on the species and context (e.g. [16, 21–24]). A study on urban trees found that tree growth was impacted not only by pruning severity but also the method of pruning [25]. In the equivalent British Standard, BS 3998:2010 *Tree Work—Recommendations*, there is a recommended general pruning limit of one third of an individual branch, although this has also been criticised for lack of a scientific basis [19].

7.4.4 Pruning or Tree Removal?

Pruning is one of the key methods by which trees can co-exist with buildings and people in urban environments. This can lead to difficult decisions around tree preservation, where an application is made to remove a protected or regulated tree and the question is asked of a court whether pruning is a satisfactory alternative to tree removal. In these cases, the purpose of pruning is typically to reduce the likelihood of future limb failure. With the assistance of expert arborist evidence, courts balance the competing concerns and apply the relevant legislation to determine the appropriate course of action.

A recent example of the decision process is set out in the South Australian case *Ditara Pty Ltd v City of Norwood et al.* [26], where the risk of harm to property or people from dropping limbs was assessed as moderate and increasing, and the likely effectiveness of pruning was found to be inadequate based on ineffective past pruning efforts. The court also looked at establishing an exclusion zone or a protective structure, finding both of these options to be unreasonable in the circumstances.

In a decision refusing permission to permit a shed to be built under a significant tree, the NSW Land and Environment Court opted for prevention by refusing the development application, rather than a path leading to inevitable future interference with the tree, such as that from pruning:

> I concur with the concerns of the ecologists and Mr Paroissien [expert arborist] that placing a dwelling under significant trees inevitably increases the amount of interference (such as pruning) with those trees. It is far preferable, if there is space to allow it, to avoid unintended consequences of interactions between trees and structures or trees and the occupants of the structures. [27, para 52]

7.5 Valuation of Amenity Trees

7.5.1 Purpose of Valuation

Valuations of urban trees are used by governments and other interested bodies to inform urban forest investment and funding decisions, or to promote a greater understanding of the value of trees to the urban community generally [28, 29]. Valuations are also used by landowners, local governments, courts and tribunals to determine appropriate tree bond amounts; determine compensation for trees removed that were improvements on land; make informed decisions on tree removal or retention; inform funding requirements for urban tree projects and planning; impose appropriate fines for unlawful tree removal; assess the added value of a tree in a land survey; or determine an appropriate insurance amount required to replace a tree.

The purpose of the valuation will largely determine the appropriate valuation method to be applied [29]. Where the purpose is for general interest or for extrapolation to a wider urban area, indirect valuation methods are often used. These methods attempt to capture the overall market value of a tree. Where the purpose is in relation to a specific individual tree (or trees), direct valuation tends to be more appropriate. This may be by way of application of a formula or using methods bespoke to the case in question. Other types of valuation measure the benefits, or ecosystem services provide by a tree on an annual basis. These methods are discussed below.

7.5.2 *Market Valuation*

As mature trees are not a good that is usually bought or sold, indirect methods of pricing are used to determine generally applicable market valuations. These indirect pricing methods are useful to underpin urban forest investment decisions and management planning, or to promote a greater understanding of the value of trees to the community generally [28]. A tree's value determined in this way can be integrated into broader valuation frameworks, for example, to input amenity values into urban forest benefit and cost analyses. These methods are therefore normally used in the context of trees on public land, such as street trees and park trees, but some assessments have extended to trees in private gardens as part of the urban forest [30]. Two of the more commonly used indirect market valuation methods are hedonic pricing and contingent valuation.

7.5.2.1 Hedonic Pricing

One indirect tree valuation method is hedonic pricing, where house sale prices are assessed for economic differences based on the presence or absence of a tree. Most hedonic pricing work on urban tree value has not differentiated between trees on public land and trees on private land. However, two studies carried out by Pandit et al. in 2013 and 2014 distinguished between trees on private own land, private neighbouring land, and adjacent public land [31, 32].

In the first study, the authors found that broadleaved trees on adjacent public land increased the property value by AU$16,889 (approximately 4.27% of the median property price) but there was no price impact of trees on private own land or private neighbouring land [31].

The second study looked at whether the tree size had any impact on hedonic values, where change in tree size was measured by canopy cover percentage. This latter study found that a 10% increase in canopy cover on adjacent public land was reflected in an increase in property price of about AU$14,500 (approximately 1.8% of the median property price). However, increases in canopy cover on private land did not increase the value of the property, with the authors finding no statistically significant positive price effect [32]. The authors surmised that the absence of a price effect on private own land (found in both studies) may reflect the disservices that fall to landowners of having trees on their property, which would negate any benefits, as well as the opportunity cost of the private land used by the tree(s) [31, 32]. Depending on the spatial parameters used, there was some indication that increases in canopy cover located on a neighbouring property actually *reduced* the relevant property price, possibly reflecting the lack of control over trees on neighbouring properties and the potential for tree disputes between neighbours [32].

7.5.2.2 Contingent Valuation

Another indirect valuation method is contingent valuation, where consumers' willingness to pay for trees is measured in economic terms to capture the value of a tree's amenity to a consumer. Contingent valuation is considered most appropriate for valuation of public non-market goods and services. This means the contingent valuation method is most often used in the context of public trees and urban forest, rather than trees on private land.[7] An interesting example of contingent valuation is demonstrated by a study assessing Florida residents' willingness to pay for urban forest invasive pest prevention (including urban forest on private land). This study found that residents were willing to pay US$5.44 per year for pest prevention, aggregating to US$540 million per year [33].

7.5.3 Formula Valuation

Direct valuation of individual amenity trees is often determined by the application of a formula leading to a monetary value for a specific tree. There are numerous different formulae that are in current use, both internationally and within Australia. Some of the better-known methods are the Helliwell Method (UK), the United States' Council of Tree and Landscape Appraisers (CTLA) and the Standard Tree Evaluation Method (STEM) developed in New Zealand. In Australia, commonly used methods include the Revised Burnley Method (developed in Victoria)[8] and the Thyer Method (developed in NSW) [34]. Due to the differing factors included and the subjective nature of many formula factors, there can be significant variation in valuation of the same tree using different formulae [35–37].

In 1973, efforts to standardise tree valuation in Australia resulted in a draft Australian Standard on Amenity Tree Value. The draft went through a number of iterations and remained unresolved for 30 years before being abandoned, setting the record for the longest running unresolved standard in Australia [38, 39]. However, Arboriculture Australia has recently developed a Minimum Industry Standard for Tree Valuation [40] for use by arborists, explaining and comparing several commonly

---

[7] However, contingent valuation has been criticised in the context of tree valuation, due to the potential for invalidating results resulting from latent non-economic factors influencing survey respondents [70].

[8] So named as a result of being developed at the Burnley Campus of the Victorian College of Agriculture and Horticulture Limited.

used valuation methods. The Minimum Industry Standard discusses the factors used in many valuation approaches and includes guidance on minimum standard criteria for any tree valuation approach. It also proposes a new valuation method (MIS506/22) designed to meet the stated minimum standard criteria.

Broadly, there are two types of valuation formula: one type estimates the cost of replacing a tree; and the other type places a value on a tree as it presently exists in the landscape.

> Any person who is attempting to place a monetary value on the amenity afforded by trees must decide whether they are looking for a figure which reflects the benefit provided by the tree (regardless of its cost) or whether they are looking for a figure which represents, in some way, the cost of planting and maintaining a tree and, if necessary, waiting several years for it to reach a significant size. These valuations will clearly not be the same in many instances. [36, p 167]

It has also been suggested that heritage trees or very large urban trees require different formulae to better reflect their significantly increased value [28, 40].

7.5.3.1 Replacement Cost Method

Replacement cost valuations are essentially based on a calculation of the volume of the mature tree multiplied by the value per square unit by reference to the nursery stock price of the same species of tree. Some methods also add care and maintenance costs to this number. Where the volume is calculated by reference to the tree's trunk, this is known as the trunk formula method. An example of this method is the CTLA Method, commonly used in the USA. In Australia, the Revised Burnley Method is similar in concept to the CTLA Method [35].

In an early comparison test of five different global methods, the Revised Burnley Method produced higher values than the formula methods used in the USA (CTLA) and the UK (Helliwell Method) [35]. In a later study comparing twelve international formula methods, the Revised Burnley Method was again among the highest valuations [37].

7.5.3.2 Compensatory Method

Methods of valuation that are based on consideration of the location, condition and other characteristics of a tree may be considered compensatory methods. These methods tend to comprise a points-based formula converted to monetary value by reference to market indicators, and involve more subjective factors than replacement cost valuation [36]. The Australian-developed Thyer Method is a compensatory value method that has been used to determine tree bond amounts [41, 42], or as evidence in a disputed tree removal application decision [43].[9] In one NSW case, involving consent orders for a development approval, the Thyer method was referenced as producing a valuation for a tree on private land of $4892, which was then imposed as a 'Tree Offset Payment' as a condition of permission to remove the tree [44].

In a valuation comparison referred to in Arboriculture Australia's Minimum Industry Standard, applying the Thyer Method and the Revised Burnley Method to a standard, mature urban tree produced remarkably similar valuations close to $60,000, despite the differences in valuation method [45].

7.5.3.3 Exceptional Trees

Some authors have suggested that most formulaic valuations are not appropriate for valuing heritage trees or very large amenity trees, as the values produced can be unrealistically low [2, 40]. The Standard Tree Evaluation Method (STEM) demonstrates the same effect but in reverse: STEM is often used in New Zealand for heritage tree valuations, but this method may not be appropriate for smaller or less significant trees, as it can produce unrealistically high values for small trees [35]. It is possible that, as one author concluded (having considered depreciation applied to amenity tree valuation), a separate valuation method should be used for exceptional amenity trees:

> The full ecological and cultural value of ancient trees may be better considered under an alternative income approach to value, since their benefits may be partly unique and irreplaceable [40, p 109]

A new formula method solely for valuation of heritage trees in compact cities has been proposed by Jim [28], with monetary values derived from property values. When tested, this method yielded average heritage tree values 66 times higher than valuation of the same trees using the CTLA Method.

7.5.4 Case-By-Case Valuation

Courts in Australia tend to rely on expert evidence of a tree's compensatory value and/or its replacement cost to inform assessment of appropriate damages to be awarded or other monetary components of a judgement, such as a tree bond amount. Some experts use formula valuation methods to underpin their evidence, and these may be accepted by courts where they are found to be appropriate for the case. However, more often courts tend to avoid formula valuation methods and prefer to make valuation assessments based on the specific circumstances of a case. This is important because one of the problems with formula valuation methods is that they are by

[9] In *Senanayake v Parramatta City Council* [43], the tree's value was referred to by the court in the context of the values listed under the Thyer Method assessment, and by the comparative value of the garage constructed nearby, but the valuation amount was not mentioned in the judgement.

nature general and lack attachment to a particular perspective. For example, if a tree creates a privacy and noise screen, that may be viewed positively by one person but the same tree blocking solar light or a view could be perceived negatively by another person [46, 47]. Courts are often undertaking a tree valuation exercise to determine a monetary amount that will properly compensate a particular person for their loss, so that person's perspective will be relevant to the valuation, but will not necessarily translate directly to a loss suffered by another person. This point was described by His Honour Justice Forrest in *Thomas v Powercor Australia Ltd* [48], where the disputed use of the Revised Burnley Method was discussed in an insurance case requiring valuation of the loss by bushfire of 35 amenity trees and shrubs. The case was one of a class of similar actions resulting from the fire. His Honour stated:

> In the event that I am persuaded that RBM [Revised Burnley Method] is the appropriate method to value Mr Thomas' loss of amenity, it does not follow that it is an appropriate measure of the loss for other properties. Much depends upon the location of the trees and plants, the actual amenity provided to the home and its occupants and several other considerations. In other words, it is simply not possible to make any binding order as to the appropriateness of RBM on a total class basis. The reality is that the assessment of this loss will need to be dealt with on a case by case basis, applying appropriate valuation methods which may differ from case to case. [48, para 18]

In *Roads Corporation v Love* [49], another Victorian Supreme Court case, a claim for compensation for land compulsorily acquired included a claim for the amount of $175,990 for the loss of 125 trees. This aspect of the claim was dismissed, with the Court finding the Revised Burnley Method (or any separate valuation of trees) to be inappropriate for cases where the trees are essentially a fixture on the land such that their value is incorporated in the market value of the land.[10]

In a case involving the unlawful destruction of three mature trees on private land by a neighbour, the District Court of Western Australia found that the lost trees were not practically able to be replaced by transplanted mature trees (as sought by the plaintiffs), instead awarding damages encompassing both the loss of amenity and the cost of revegetation. The Court, relying upon expert evidence, awarded damages of $25,000 for replacement and care of new trees and shrubs, and $15,000 for lost amenity [50].

7.5.5 *Benefits and Services Valuation*

As tree provide multiple benefits over their lifespan, calculating the value of those benefits on an annual or whole-of-life basis is another way to value urban trees in monetary terms. Often described as ecosystem services, research has been undertaken to categorise and value some of the benefits or services provided by urban trees and forests [51]. Translation of the benefits from urban trees into economic terms is

---

[10] Similar findings have been made by the Supreme Court of Western Australia [71] and the State Administrative Tribunal of Western Australia [72].

continuing to be researched and assessed, as this area of research is complex and relatively new [52].

7.5.5.1 Ecosystem Services

According to Croci et al. [53], in a study reviewing literature on urban ecosystems, it is realistic to discern 13 ecosystem services applicable to urban ecosystems, including biodiversity services. Valuing each of these services is complex, because each service requires one or more methods of value assessment appropriate to the benefit generated by the service. For example, pollution removal is an ecosystem service that provides cleaner air and may be valued by measuring the health care cost savings that result [52]; whereas a tree's contribution to local climate regulation (another ecosystem service) results in cooler temperatures that may be valued (in part) by measuring the household energy costs saved [53, 54].

A commonly used method for assessing ecosystem services benefits of trees is the iTree Eco Method, a set of tools within the iTree software package that provides pre-set equations for assessing and valuing some ecosystem services of trees [52].

In a global literature review of valuations applied to ecosystem services at the urban level, the most commonly valued urban ecosystem services were found to be local climate regulation and air purification. The review also found that limited ecosystem services were valued in individual studies, and non-use values (such as providing a sense of place) were rarely included, indicating a general tendency to underestimate the value of urban ecosystem services [53].

Although most ecosystem services valuations of urban trees are aimed at assessing the wider urban forest, some valuations have been applied to individual trees on private land. For example, a 2023 study to compare urban tree replacement value assessment and ecosystem services assessment included a category of trees described as trees in multi-family residential areas in Warsaw, Poland, which were noted to be often in private ownership. The study assessed the ecosystem services (air purification only) value of residential trees to be US$15 per tree per year and the replacement value (trunk formula method) of the same residential trees to be US$1,602 per tree. In both valuation types, the residential trees were valued more highly than street trees, but lower than park trees [55].

7.5.5.2 Cost and Benefit Analyses

Valuation of the benefits provided by urban trees will not provide a complete economic picture unless the disservices and costs of tree maintenance are also considered. A study reviewing the ecosystem *disservices* of urban trees (such as damage to property and littering) found that such disservices were rarely included in valuations, whilst acknowledging that many disservices are linked to management activities and associated management costs [56].

A recent, detailed overview of the benefits and costs of urban forest ecosystems has been set out in a book chapter by Nowak and Dwyer [57]. The authors discuss current valuation methods for all the ecosystem services of trees, along with the balancing disservices and costs. Some of the complexities of benefit cost analyses referred to include substantial differences in the benefits of trees depending on their precise location, and the perspective that is chosen, as the person gaining the benefit may be different to the person suffering the cost or disservice.

A review of global urban forest cost and benefit valuation literature found that in most studies reviewed, the benefits were found to outweigh the costs, and that the 'aesthetic and amenity' value component was typically the highest value benefit [30]. An Australian example of this effect may be found in the CSIRO and the ACT Government analysis of the ACT public urban forest [58], undertaken to provide alternative cost and benefit options for differing levels of canopy cover over time. The analysis involved valuation of seven ecosystem services benefits, finding that the flow of ecosystem services from the public urban forest was worth $27.12 million in 2018. The largest component of this amount related to property premium land rates estimates (just over $14 million), as property values would be increased by the existence of verge trees. The premium valuation was based on the hedonic pricing of verge trees study by Pandit et al. [31] as discussed above. In other words, this was the amenity value component.[11]

7.5.5.3 Impact of Future Scarcity on Valuation

The continuing decrease in overall abundance of trees in urban areas, especially peri-urban forested areas lost as a result of urbanisation, leads to increased scarcity in ecosystem services, including those linked to biodiversity values.[12] For example, the banksia woodlands in the Perth and Peel area of Western Australia are within a global biodiversity hotspot and are a vulnerable ecological community, predominantly impacted by urban expansion. Due to their resultant scarcity, the banksia woodlands are now listed as a Threatened Ecological Community under federal environmental law [59] and have become a focus of conservation efforts by locals, including Indigenous people [60].

There is research to suggest that urban residents' level of contact with nature has a positive correlation to their willingness to pay for its preservation [61]. In theory, it would follow that, where there is a decline in urban residents' direct contact with nature, willingness to pay to protect nature may accordingly reduce with that decline. However, some authors consider that environmental scarcity, as with other goods and services, results in an increased willingness to pay, which should be reflected in the

[11] Another interesting aspect of the analysis was the whole-of-life costs per tree, which were split between costs of native and non-native (exotic) trees, with exotic trees costing $8.41 annually per tree, more than double that of native trees at $3.07 [58].

[12] Biodiversity may be seen both as indirectly supporting and facilitating other ecosystem services, and as providing a direct ecosystem service whereby people obtain value from the existence and quality of biodiversity [73].

valuation of ecosystem services in order to correct a substantial downward bias in current ecosystem services valuations [62].

7.6 Conclusion

The matters discussed in this chapter highlight some of the factors relevant to private landowner decision-making around tree retention. Where trees are often valuable assets from a community perspective, there are common key factors present in heightened value of trees: the tree's size, health and location are three of the most significant factors [55]. These factors can be improved by the use of Australian Standards designed to minimise the risk of tree injury or death in urban environments. However, the costs of retaining trees (and in particular large, healthy trees in urban locations) on private land typically fall entirely to individual landowners.

The economic rationale behind decision making of individual landowners with trees, seen as a hybrid private/public good, may be a type of 'tragedy of the commons', in the sense that the cost to each individual can be seen to outweigh the individual benefits, and so the benefits to the wider community are destroyed when the individual decision is reached the remove a tree [63]. As observed with some prescience by Llewellyn in 1984, when discussing protection of private amenity trees in NSW:

> It seems clear that in this case of "amenity protection", and in other similar areas, the measurable costs to individuals of preserving that amenity against the "immeasurable" benefit of the community or group is a powerful mechanism for incremental environmental destruction [64, p 181]

For this reason, it is important to understand the costs and benefits as perceived and experienced by private landowners with urban trees: however, this area is under-researched. Costs may include not only management costs and increased construction costs, but also the opportunity cost of using the land to retain a tree, and other anxiety-producing concerns such as personal safety and potential neighbour disputes [31]. Further research to understand landowner perspectives on the benefits and costs of tree ownership could provide valuable information on ways to encourage tree retention on private land.

References

1. Piovesan G, Biondi F (2021) On tree longevity. New Phytol 231:1318–1337. https://doi.org/10.1111/nph.17148
2. Price C (2021) Further considerations concerning CAVAT. Arboric J 43:215–234
3. Boyd v Woollahra Municipal Council [2024] NSWLEC 1398
4. Cooper J (1996) Legislation to protect and replace trees on private land: Ordinances in Westchester County, New York. Arboric Urban For 22:270–278. https://doi.org/10.48044/jauf.1996.041

5. Koeser A, Hauer R, Norris K, Krouse R (2013) Factors influencing long-term street tree survival in Milwaukee, WI, USA. Urban For Urban Green 12:562–568. https://doi.org/10.1016/j.ufug.2013.05.006
6. Hauer RJ, Koeser AK, Parbs S et al (2020) Long-term effects and development of a tree preservation program on tree condition, survival, and growth. Landsc Urban Plan 193:103670. https://doi.org/10.1016/j.landurbplan.2019.103670
7. O'Herrin K, Hauer R, Pike K, Vogt J (2022) Homebuilder activities and knowledge of tree preservation during construction: comparison of practitioners in rural and urban locations. Sustainability 14:2753. https://doi.org/10.3390/su14052753
8. Pike K, O'Herrin K, Klimas C, Vogt J (2021) Tree preservation during construction: an evaluation of a comprehensive municipal tree ordinance. Urban For Urban Green 57:126914. https://doi.org/10.1016/j.ufug.2020.126914
9. Ordóñez-Barona C, Bush J, Hurley J et al (2021) International approaches to protecting and retaining trees on private urban land. J Environ Manage 285:112081. https://doi.org/10.1016/j.jenvman.2021.112081
10. Australian Capital Territory Government (2023) Urban Forest Act 2023 (ACT)
11. Australian Capital Territory Government (2023) Urban Forest Regulation 2023 (ACT)
12. CPDM Pty Ltd v North Sydney Council [2024] NSWLEC 1262
13. Harris v Waverley Council [2024] NSWLEC 1306
14. Hunters Hill Council v Johnston [2013] NSWLEC 89
15. Mirvac Projects Ltd v Ku-ring-gai Council [2005] NSWLEC 504
16. Kane B (2017) Pruning. In: Ferrini F, Konijnendijk van den Bosch CC, Fini A (eds) Routledge handbook of urban forestry, 1st ed. Taylor & Francis Group, pp 407–418
17. Morris H (2010) Tree pruning: A brief history. Int Dendrol Soc 217–225
18. Shigo AL (1983) Tree Defects: A Photo Guide. U.S. Department of Agriculture, Forest Service, Northeastern Forest Experiment Station
19. Morris H (2013) Tree pruning: A modern approach. Int Dendrol Soc 209
20. South Australian Government (2017) Planning, Development and Infrastructure (General) Regulations 2017. South Australia
21. Clark JR, Matheny N (2010) The research foundation to tree pruning: A review of the literature. Arboric Urban For 36:110–120
22. Alcorn PJ, Bauhus J, Smith RGB et al (2008) Growth response following green crown pruning in plantation-grown *Eucalyptus pilularis* and *Eucalyptus cloeziana*. Can J For Res 38:770–781. https://doi.org/10.1139/X07-185
23. Pinkard EA (2003) Physiological and growth responses related to pattern and severity of green pruning in young Eucalyptus globulus. For Ecol Manage 182:231–245. https://doi.org/10.1016/S0378-1127(03)00046-X
24. Pinkard EA (2002) Effects of pattern and severity of pruning on growth and branch development of pre-canopy closure Eucalyptus nitens. For Ecol Manage 157:217–230. https://doi.org/10.1016/S0378-1127(00)00647-2
25. Fini A, Frangi P, Faoro M et al (2015) Effects of different pruning methods on an urban tree species: A four-year-experiment scaling down from the whole tree to the chloroplasts. Urban For Urban Green 14:664–674. https://doi.org/10.1016/j.ufug.2015.06.011
26. Ditara Pty Ltd v City of Norwood, Payneham and St Peters Council Assessment Panel [2024] SAERDC 14
27. Wang v Willoughby City Council [2012] NSWLEC 1328
28. Jim CY (2006) Formulaic expert method to integrate evaluation and valuation of heritage trees in compact city. Environ Monit Assess 116:53–80. https://doi.org/10.1007/s10661-006-7245-x
29. Price C (2007) Putting a value on trees: an economist's perspective. Arboric J 30:7–19. https://doi.org/10.1080/03071375.2007.9747474
30. Song XP, Tan PY, Edwards P, Richards D (2018) The economic benefits and costs of trees in urban forest stewardship: a systematic review. Urban For Urban Green 29:162–170
31. Pandit R, Polyakov M, Tapsuwan S, Moran T (2013) The effect of street trees on property value in Perth, Western Australia. Landsc Urban Plan 110:134–142. https://doi.org/10.1016/j.landurbplan.2012.11.001

32. Pandit R, Polyakov M, Sadler R (2014) Valuing public and private urban tree canopy cover. Aust J Agric Resour Econ 58:453–470. https://doi.org/10.1111/1467-8489.12037
33. Adams DC, Soto JR, Lai J et al (2020) Public preferences and willingness to pay for invasive forest pest prevention programs in urban areas. Forests 11:1056. https://doi.org/10.3390/f11101056
34. Thyer P (2002) Introduction to the Thyer Tree Valuation Method—Worksheet. https://www.peterthyer.com/Thyer%20Tree%20Valuation%20introduction%20Jan%202002.pdf. Accessed 24 Aug 2024
35. Watson G (2002) Comparing formula methods of tree appraisal. J Arboric 28:11–18
36. Helliwell R (2008) Amenity valuation of trees and woodlands. Arboric J 31:161–168. https://doi.org/10.1080/03071375.2008.9747532
37. Ponce-Donoso M, Vallejos-Barra Ó, Escobedo F (2017) Appraisal of urban trees using twelve valuation formulas and two appraiser groups. Arboric Urban For 43. https://doi.org/10.48044/jauf.2017.007
38. Moore GM (2006) Urban tree valuation—a current perspective and progress report. In: The 7th National Street Tree Symposium
39. Moore G (2018) Tree protection Australian standards and the law: Getting it right. Treenet
40. Hollis A (2009) Can trees be depreciated like (mechanical) plant? A depreciated replacement cost solution to the adjusted trunk formula anomaly in CTLA'S trunk formula method. Arboric J 32:97–110. https://doi.org/10.1080/03071375.2009.9747561
41. Klompe v Woollahra Municipal Council [2009] NSWLEC 1071
42. IUS Pty Ltd v Woollahra Municipal Council [2006] NSWLEC 690
43. Senanayake v Parramatta City Council [2007] NSWLEC 170
44. Hurstville Community Centre Inc v Georges River Council [2022] NSWLEC 1468
45. Strauss S (2022) MIS506 tree valuation : Industry guidance on tree valuation methodologies, practices and standards. Arboriculture Australia and New Zealand Arboricultural Association Inc.
46. Cimburova Z, Blumentrath S, Barton DN (2023) Making trees visible: A GIS method and tool for modelling visibility in the valuation of urban trees. Urban For Urban Green 81:127839. https://doi.org/10.1016/j.ufug.2023.127839
47. Lyytimäki J, Petersen LK, Normander B, Bezák P (2008) Nature as a nuisance? Ecosystem services and disservices to urban lifestyle. Environ Sci (Ruse) 5:161–172. https://doi.org/10.1080/15693430802055524
48. Thomas v Powercor Australia Ltd (No 5) [2011] VSC 482
49. Roads Corporation v Love [2013] VSC 176
50. Blythe v Hamblin [2009] WADC 192
51. Chen WY, Jim CY (2008) Assessment and valuation of the ecosystem services provided by urban forests. In: Carreiro MM, Song YC (eds) Ecology, planning, and management of urban forests. Springer, New York, NY, pp 53–83
52. Nowak DJ (2021) Understanding i-Tree: 2021 summary of programs and methods. US Department of Agriculture, Forest Service. https://doi.org/10.2737/NRS-GTR-200-2021
53. Croci E, Lucchitta B, Penati T (2021) Valuing ecosystem services at the urban level: a critical review. Sustainability 13:1129. https://doi.org/10.3390/su13031129
54. Pandit R, Laband DN (2010) Energy savings from tree shade. Ecol Econ 69:1324–1329. https://doi.org/10.1016/j.ecolecon.2010.01.009
55. Suchocka M, Heciak J, Błaszczyk M et al (2023) Comparison of ecosystem services and replacement value calculations performed for urban trees. Ecosyst Serv 63:101553. https://doi.org/10.1016/j.ecoser.2023.101553
56. Roman LA, Conway TM, Eisenman TS et al (2021) Beyond 'trees are good': Disservices, management costs, and tradeoffs in urban forestry. Ambio 50:615–630. https://doi.org/10.1007/s13280-020-01396-8
57. Nowak DJ, Dwyer JF (2007) Understanding the benefits and costs of urban forest ecosystems. In: Kuser JE (ed) Urban and community forestry in the northeast. Springer, Netherlands, Dordrecht, pp 25–46

58. Tapsuwan S, Marcos-Martinez R, Schandl H (2019) An environmental-economic accounting of services provided by the living infrastructure in the ACT: Public urban forests and irrigated open spaces. Canberra, ACT
59. Australian Government (1999) Environment Protection and Biodiversity Conservation Act 1999 (Cth). Australia
60. Ritchie AL, Svejcar LN, Ayre BM et al (2021) Corrigendum to: A threatened ecological community: Research advances and priorities for Banksia woodlands. Aust J Bot 69:111. https://doi.org/10.1071/BT20089_CO
61. Sato M, Aoshima I, Chang Y (2021) Connectedness to nature and the conservation of the urban ecosystem: Perspectives from the valuation of urban forests. For Policy Econ 125:102396. https://doi.org/10.1016/j.forpol.2021.102396
62. Drupp MA, Hänsel MC, Fenichel EP, et al (2024) Accounting for the increasing benefits from scarce ecosystems. Science (1979) 383:1062–1064. https://doi.org/10.1126/science.adk2086
63. Hardin G (1968) The tragedy of the commons. Science (1979) 162:1243–1248. https://doi.org/10.1126/science.162.3859.1243
64. Llewellyn J (1984) Tree preservation orders in New South Wales: Some legal and economic aspects. Environmental and Planning Law Journal 1:178
65. Watson GW (1998) Tree growth after trenching and compensatory crown pruning. J Arboric 24:47–53
66. Benson AR, Koeser AK, Morgenroth J (2019) A test of tree protection zones: Responses of Quercus virginiana Mill trees to root severance treatments. Urban For Urban Green 38:54–63. https://doi.org/10.1016/j.ufug.2018.10.015
67. Day S, Wiseman PE, Dickinson S, Harris JR (2010) Contemporary concepts of root system architecture of urban trees. Arboric Urban For 36:149–159. https://doi.org/10.48044/jauf.2010.020
68. Fini A, Frangi P, Mori J et al (2020) Evaluating the effects of trenching on growth, physiology and uprooting resistance of two urban tree species over 51-months. Urban For Urban Green 53:126734. https://doi.org/10.1016/j.ufug.2020.126734
69. Newbury District Council v Secretary of State for the Environment [1981] AC 578
70. Lo AY, Jim CY (2015) Protest response and willingness to pay for culturally significant urban trees: Implications for contingent valuation method. Ecol Econ 114:58–66. https://doi.org/10.1016/j.ecolecon.2015.03.012
71. Lenz Nominees Pty Ltd v Commissioner of Main Roads [2012] WASC 6
72. Avila v Main Roads Western Australia [2023] WASAT 79
73. Paul C, Hanley N, Meyer ST, et al (2020) On the functional relationship between biodiversity and economic value. Sci Adv 6. https://doi.org/10.1126/sciadv.aax7712

Chapter 8
Conclusion

Abstract The protection of trees on private urban land in Australia is complicated by the wide array of mechanisms that impact each part of the full cycle of tree growth, health and death. Authors in this field operate within different disciplines and naturally bring differing perspectives on the underlying issues. This review has allowed a unique opportunity to consider the broad themes that emerge from author perspectives across this topic. Some authors consider that a shift is required in how Australians think about urban living (in particular the Australian Dream); others take the view that the existing controls can and will work but need only adjustment in the applied parameters; while a third theme sees authors advocating for economic controls designed to shift existing patterns. Over time, the urban forest would benefit from landowners, developers and governments paying greater attention to ensuring the right tree is planted in the right location and has everything it needs to thrive, including deep soil, light, space and protections that will hold fast until the end of its natural role in the urban ecosystem.

8.1 The Importance of Trees on Private Land

This review set out to explore, in a holistic way, the mechanisms that directly and indirectly influence urban trees on private land in Australia, to gain a better understanding of the existing framework and mechanisms that contribute to the decline of canopy cover on private land.

It is clear that local government canopy cover goals will be difficult (if not impossible) to meet if they do not include canopy cover on private land [1, 2]. In addition to their key role in supporting urban canopy cover goals, trees on private urban land also provide a particularly important role in improving the quality of urban life, including mitigating the urban heat island effect [3], providing biodiversity support [4, 5], assisting regulation of stormwater [4, 7, 8], reducing energy consumption [9], and improving health and wellbeing [10]. Private urban trees can also help establish

E. J. Scaife, *Urban Tree Protection on Private Land*,
SpringerBriefs in Law, https://doi.org/10.1007/978-981-95-1857-9_8

a connection with nature, which is an important element in the cycle of stewardship, and this can be forgotten as something that can happen within cities.[1]

Certain factors can make a difference to the level of impact on each of these benefits. For example, the cooling effect of urban trees is highly linked to their canopies, with variables including the crown cover and density of the trees [11]. Water regulation, particularly reducing water use, is best achieved by species that are drought tolerant. Native planting and increased understorey cover can improve biodiversity outcomes [4]. The impact of trees on energy efficiency in buildings depends on a number of factors, including the location of the tree relative to the building and the height of the tree [9].

Planning an urban forest that encompasses private land may therefore need to go further than encouraging, or even requiring, more trees to be planted and retained. There may also be a need to find ways to shape the private urban forest, over time, to best meet the needs of current and future generations.

8.2 Emerging Themes

This review has revealed broad themes for solutions that are repeated by authors across many of the problem areas upon which research has focussed. The themes can be grouped into three distinct categories. One theme maintains that the problems stem from a particular way of thinking and that a perspective or cultural shift will be required to make a real difference. Another theme maintains that the existing system merely needs adjustment: tighter controls, stricter enforcement, and legislative priorities to be set in favour of trees. A third theme is focussed on economic aspects: if trees were to be valued more highly in the economy, or to be a part of the least expensive way of achieving goals, behavioural changes will follow naturally and canopy cover on private land would improve as a consequence.

8.2.1 A Shift in Perspective

Some authors considering the problem of declining urban trees on private land have pointed to entrenched perspectives which, if changed, would allow the generating of solutions that are presently unthinkable. Two key mindset shifts that have arisen in this review are discussed briefly below.

[1] For example, the Australian Urban Strategy prepared by the Commonwealth Government omits to mention connection with nature that can happen in cities, only covering this impact in relation to natural areas outside of cities.

8.2.1.1 Stewardship of Urban Trees

To properly enhance the protection of urban trees, there is growing evidence that there needs to be a paradigm shift, towards a sense of stewardship of urban trees on private land [12, 13]. In a broader sense, this may be seen as a step towards the 'unthinkable' possibility postulated by Christopher Stone, in his seminal 1972 article '*Should Trees Have Standing?*' [14], that trees could—and should—have certain rights that are safeguarded by society. Research addressing the need for stewardship focuses on mechanisms designed to support this shift, for example the provision of incentives to landowners to retain or plant trees [12], the need for education about the benefits of trees [13], understanding the relationships between urban residents and private trees [15], and encouraging a connection with trees and nature [16], particularly for children [17].

8.2.1.2 Changing the Australian Dream

The Australian Dream is said to be the desire to live in your own detached family home with a backyard [18]. Some authors credit the existence of the Australian Dream with driving the creation of a monotonous supply of urban housing that repeatedly preferences house over garden when block sizes are smaller [18, 19]. In this way, an attachment to the Australian Dream is seen as causing shrinking gardens, and with it, shrinking urban canopy cover. According to a recent study, the Australian Dream remains disappointingly alive, underpinning a poor outlook for the future of urban sustainability [19]. These authors believe that a perspective shift is required for Australians to let go of—or change—the Australian Dream and embrace higher density living in a variety of forms, allowing sprawling mid-density gardenless suburbs to shift towards more sustainable housing types [15, 19, 20].

8.2.2 Tighter Controls

As many of the existing controls that impact urban canopy cover are set using specific parameters, it is perhaps the simplest approach to merely change the parameters whilst leaving the existing controls intact. Authors examining the problems associated with specific controls often suggest ways in which those controls could be tightened or better managed for a greater impact. The key areas of research on increased controls relate to stricter tree retention mechanisms [21, 22], adjusting planning regulations to create more private open space when new houses are constructed [20, 23], and adjusting planning regulations to increase public open space in both greenfield developments and infill developments [24, 25].

There appears to be considerable scope for changes of this type, which could increase canopy cover on private land without the need for significant changes in existing legislative frameworks. For example, this is the general approach taken in the Parliamentary Inquiry carried out in South Australia, which provides several suggestions for minor changes, that, taken together, may make a significant difference to canopy cover [22]. However, it is apparent that a problem with bringing many of these suggested changes into effect is the policy conflict between the need for urban trees and the need for more housing, particularly affordable housing. This conflict presents as a key issue for many state governments (and sometime local governments), whereby tighter controls to support urban trees may be simply refused on the basis that such change might inhibit housing supply.

8.2.3 It's All About Money

Some researchers take the view that valuation of the ecosystem services provided by urban trees is critical as it translates the benefits of trees into monetary units, that can then be compared with alternatives in decision making [26] or integrated into other urban programs [27]. The use of 'nature-based solutions' [28] is gaining attention globally, particularly in Europe [29, 30], with the aim of increasing public and private investment in nature-based solutions as a key component of transformational change [31]. At present, ecosystem services of urban trees that relate to water regulation and cooling are of particular interest in Australian cities, as drought and heat are significant urban problems resulting from climate change [32, 33]. Where future government spending may be needed to address these issues, valuation of the relevant ecosystem services of urban trees could underpin investment in the urban forest, rather than investment in grey infrastructure. Alternatively, others have suggested that a system of ongoing payment for ecosystems services could also fund investment in the urban forest [34].

Researchers have also considered economic approaches to drive landowner behaviour in several different contexts in this review, which some see as a way to resolve the policy conflict between housing supply and tighter controls [35]. Various types of economic incentive have been applied by governments, including tax incentives and biodiversity offset payments for conservation covenants [36] and the provision of other indirect economic benefits in return for tree retention such as a reduction in the required deep soil contribution for new development [37, 38]. Researchers have also suggested that economic benefits for building smaller houses could be beneficial, such as such as taxation, financing models and support for innovative housing provision [35].

8.3 Further Research

With a focus on mechanisms to increase canopy on private urban land, the insights gained from this review have highlighted particular areas that future academic research could usefully address.

8.3.1 Strengthening Tree Retention Laws

Existing tree retention laws, comprising blanket protections and significant tree registers, are utilised by many local governments around Australia. However, given the wide variation in local laws, it is not clear whether there are any examples of these mechanisms working well, or how they could be most effectively improved. If tree retention mechanisms are to be improved, it will be important to identify the strongest and weakest components of existing laws. Two components of tree retention that have been the subject of little research to date are enforcement (both in terms of the applicable fines and level of active enforcement by local government) and the practical effect of exemptions and exclusions. A better understanding of the general impacts of tree protection policies on landowners could help improve local government engagement with landowners.

8.3.2 Landowner Views on Bearing Responsibility for Private Trees

The costs of ownership of private trees are borne largely by the landowner and may include consideration of concerns such as the opportunity cost of retaining a tree and personal safety risks [39]. Further research to understand landowner perspectives on the benefits, costs and perceived risks of tree ownership could provide valuable information on ways to encourage tree retention on private land.

This review has been conducted with several limitations (as set out in Chap. 1), one of which is the decision not to address the topic of neighbour disputes over urban trees. However, one author has noted that neighbour disputes may have a potential negative impact on the value of a tree on private land. Future research should include this topic in the context of exploring landowner views on bearing the responsibility for trees on private land.

8.3.3 Landowner Engagement in Conservation of Peri-Urban Land

Peri-urban land (or the urban 'fringe') has been highlighted as of particular importance in urban planning because its continuing loss reduces human contact with nature and causes several negative environmental impacts [40], effects that are not necessarily mitigated by offsets [41]. There is evidence that some landowners of peri-urban land may choose to not conserve the land for the long term as they wish to be able to take advantage of a future change in land use that could add value to the land. Conservation of private land in peri-urban areas could be enhanced by better understanding the reasons for landowner engagement in conservation measures and considering potential regulatory measures or incentives that could assist landowners to conserve native vegetation in such areas.

8.3.4 Re-thinking Public Open Space Provision

Many questions have been raised in the literature about the adequacy and appropriateness of public open space provision, particularly the contributions required from developers. However, governments appear constrained by the prospect that legislating for increased public open space contributions will result in reduced housing supply and less affordable housing. For this debate to move forward, further research examining how to integrate better provision of public open space with increased housing supply would be useful.

One approach worth further consideration is the application of environmental infrastructure either as stand-alone infrastructure or in place of other types of infrastructure, particularly grey infrastructure for water regulation [32, 42, 43]. For example, could the USA experience of using green infrastructure to solve water quality issues be effective in Australian cities?

Another approach is whether a system of payment for urban ecosystem services could provide funding to support future urban ecosystem management [34]. Further exploration of this possibility would also be beneficial.

8.3.5 Provision for Garden Space When New Homes Are Built

As housing density is negatively correlated with private open space [44], various mechanisms have been suggested to increase the garden space in new housing developments and infill housing. Future research could examine which of the proposed options would be most effective in creating garden space, and which would be most desirable from the perspective of landowners and developers. From this review, the options suggested by various authors include:

- Increasing existing setback requirements and reducing the allowable footprint of a new house [20];
- Imposing general principles that differ for small lot infill and larger precinct scale developments:
  - o for small lot subdivision, planning mechanisms enforced by local government designed to ensure that each small lot decision works towards the incremental improvement of urban nature; and

  - o for precinct scale developments, site layouts arranged to maximise onsite green infrastructure, including deep soil zones and setbacks, and buildings designed to integrate urban greenery in, on and over built form [45].

- Encouraging reduction of new house sizes by methods such as taxation, new financing models and support for innovative housing provision [35].
- Changing the way new greenfield developments presently work, to require developers to also be responsible for the construction of homes, allowing for economies of scale and improved housing design that includes more sustainable elements including trees and additional garden space [20];
- Considering whether requirements for car parking, hard stands and driveways could be reduced or eliminated for many homes, possibly by engaging a transit-oriented development approach [46] or increasing connectivity of green space for active transport [47, 48], and how the resultant space might be used for private urban trees and green space.

In considering any mechanism designed to create more garden space, some authors raise a need to consider the risks of negative outcomes from green gentrification (see Chap. 5). It is possible that mechanisms maintaining housing affordability whist increasing garden space could reduce the likelihood that green gentrification would have anything more than a negligible impact.

8.3.6 Health Related Benefits of Urban Trees

The mental and physical health related benefits of urban trees are the subject of considerable and increasing attention in the literature. Where state and territory governments have responsibility for both health and planning, synergies between the two areas could be more easily implemented. The present focus on the cooling effect of urban trees and the links to heat-related concerns for health (including morbidity) and the economic outcomes could add to the financial consideration of investment in urban trees including incentives for landowners to retain or plant trees that are particularly beneficial for cooling impacts.

Further valuation of the health benefits of urban trees could be helpful in creating comparisons of approaches and expenditure, helping to ensure that urban forest planning considers the ways that trees on private land can have the greatest impact in areas where they are most needed.

8.3.7 Communication with Landowners

Urban residents' experiences related to garden trees is important in their decision making about trees [15]. A study reviewing landowners' reasons for planting trees found that beautification and biodiversity support were among the top reasons given

[49]. In addition, planting on private land is tending to favour smaller trees, with fewer large trees being planted [50]. It is likely that government communication with private landowners and urban residents about benefits, impacts and policies relevant to urban trees is an important part of changing community behaviours.

> Even poorly designed and enforced regulatory programmes appear to increase in effectiveness when they successfully communicate with the public and obtain public support. [51, at p 187]

Further research to identify ways of creating successful communications between urban residents and policy makers about benefits and management of private urban trees would be valuable.

8.4 Concluding Comment

Upon learning that private land is considered to be the key area of difficulty with achieving goals of increasing urban canopy cover, I resolved to take up the research challenge of investigating the policies and mechanisms that were working against urban canopy increase, as suggested by Hurley et al. [52].

I hope that this review addresses that challenge by presenting a detailed yet accessible investigation of the current policies and mechanism that impact the urban forest on private land, and provides a useful foundation for future work to support the development of effective mechanisms to increase and improve the urban forest in Australia.

References

1. Torquato PR, Szota C, Hahs AK et al (2025) Insufficient space: Prioritizing large tree species and planting designs still fail to meet urban forest canopy targets. Landsc Urban Plan 256:105287. https://doi.org/10.1016/j.landurbplan.2024.105287
2. Marcos Martinez R, Soonsawad N, Dias Baptista M et al (2025) Challenges and strategies in meeting urban tree canopy targets: A scenario discovery analysis to guide urban forest planning in new developments. Trees, Forests and People 19:100787. https://doi.org/10.1016/j.tfp.2025.100787
3. Yenneti K, Ding L, Prasad D et al (2020) Urban overheating and cooling potential in Australia: An evidence-based review. Climate 8:126. https://doi.org/10.3390/cli8110126
4. Threlfall CG, Mata L, Mackie JA et al (2017) Increasing biodiversity in urban green spaces through simple vegetation interventions. J Appl Ecol 54:1874–1883. https://doi.org/10.1111/1365-2664.12876
5. Ordóñez C, Threlfall CG, Kendal D et al (2023) Quantifying the importance of urban trees to people and nature through tree removal experiments. People and Nature 5:1316–1335. https://doi.org/10.1002/pan3.10509
6. Grey V, Livesley SJ, Fletcher TD, Szota C (2018) Tree pits to help mitigate runoff in dense urban areas. J Hydrol (Amst) 565:400–410. https://doi.org/10.1016/j.jhydrol.2018.08.038

7. Berland A, Shiflett SA, Shuster WD et al (2017) The role of trees in urban stormwater management. Landsc Urban Plan 162:167–177. https://doi.org/10.1016/j.landurbplan.2017.02.017
8. Yang L, Zhang L, Li Y, Wu S (2015) Water-related ecosystem services provided by urban green space: A case study in Yixing City (China). Landsc Urban Plan 136:40–51. https://doi.org/10.1016/j.landurbplan.2014.11.016
9. Rouhollahi M, Whaley D, Byrne J, Boland J (2022) Potential residential tree arrangement to optimise dwelling energy efficiency. Energy Build 261:111962. https://doi.org/10.1016/j.enbuild.2022.111962
10. Wolf KL, Lam ST, McKeen JK et al (2020) Urban trees and human health: a scoping review. Int J Environ Res Public Health 17:4371. https://doi.org/10.3390/ijerph17124371
11. Balany F, Ng AW, Muttil N et al (2020) Green infrastructure as an urban heat island mitigation strategy—a review. Water (Basel) 12:3577. https://doi.org/10.3390/w12123577
12. Ordóñez-Barona C, Bush J, Hurley J et al (2021) International approaches to protecting and retaining trees on private urban land. J Environ Manage 285:112081
13. Clark C, Ordonez C, Livesley SJ (2020) Private tree removal, public loss: Valuing and enforcing existing tree protection mechanisms is the key to retaining urban trees on private land. Landsc Urban Plan 203. https://doi.org/10.1016/j.landurbplan.2020.103899
14. Stone CD (1972) Should trees have standing?—towards legal rights for natural objects. South Calif Law Rev 45:450–501
15. Pearce LM, Davison A, Kirkpatrick JB (2015) Personal encounters with trees: The lived significance of the private urban forest. Urban For Urban Green 14:1–7. https://doi.org/10.1016/j.ufug.2014.11.003
16. de Kleyn L, Mumaw L, Corney H (2020) From green spaces to vital places: connection and expression in urban greening. Aust Geogr 51:205–219. https://doi.org/10.1080/00049182.2019.1686195
17. Rupprecht CDD, Byrne JA, Lo AY (2016) Memories of vacant lots: How and why residents used informal urban green space as children and teenagers in Brisbane, Australia, and Sapporo, Japan. Child Geogr 14:340–355. https://doi.org/10.1080/14733285.2015.1048427
18. Walters P (2021) The vanishing suburban dream in Australia. disP—The Planning Review 57:4–21. https://doi.org/10.1080/02513625.2021.2026646
19. Willing R, Pojani D (2017) Is the suburban dream still alive in Australia? Evidence from Brisbane. Australian Planner 54:67–79. https://doi.org/10.1080/07293682.2017.1296875
20. Hall T (2010) The life and death of the Australian Backyard. CSIRO Publishing, Collingwood
21. Belder RL, Delaporte KD, Caddy-Retalic S (2022) Urban tree protection in Australia: Review of regulatory matters. University of Adelaide, Adelaide
22. South Australian Parliament (2023) Inquiry into the Urban Forest—Interim Report
23. Thomson G, Newman P, Hes D et al (2022) Nature-positive design and development: A case study on regenerating black cockatoo habitat in urban developments in Perth. Australia. Urban Science 6:47. https://doi.org/10.3390/urbansci6030047
24. Grose MJ (2007) Perth's Stephenson-Hepburn Plan of 1955: 10% POS, and housing then and now. Australian planner 44:20–21. https://doi.org/10.1080/07293682.2007.9982608
25. Grose MJ (2009) Changing relationships in public open space and private open space in suburbs in south-western Australia. Landsc Urban Plan 92:53–63. https://doi.org/10.1016/j.landurbplan.2009.02.006
26. Chen WY, Jim CY (2008) Assessment and valuation of the ecosystem services provided by urban forests. In: Carreiro MM, Song YC (eds) Ecology, planning, and management of urban forests. Springer, New York, NY, pp 53–83
27. Nowak DJ (2006) Institutionalizing urban forestry as a "biotechnology" to improve environmental quality. Urban For Urban Green 5:93–100. https://doi.org/10.1016/j.ufug.2006.04.002
28. Pearlmutter D, Theochari D, Nehls T et al (2020) Enhancing the circular economy with nature-based solutions in the built urban environment: Green building materials, systems and sites. Blue-Green Systems 2:46–72. https://doi.org/10.2166/bgs.2019.928

29. Davies C, Chen WY, Sanesi G, Lafortezza R (2021) The European Union roadmap for implementing nature-based solutions: A review. Environ Sci Policy 121:49–67. https://doi.org/10.1016/j.envsci.2021.03.018
30. Lafortezza R, Chen J, van den Bosch CK, Randrup TB (2018) Nature-based solutions for resilient landscapes and cities. Environ Res 165:431–441. https://doi.org/10.1016/j.envres.2017.11.038
31. European Commission Nature-based solutions research policy. In: European Commission website. https://research-and-innovation.ec.europa.eu/research-area/environment/nature-based-solutions/research-policy_en?prefLang=bg. Accessed 4 Nov 2024
32. Legislative Assembly Environment and Planning Committee (2022) Inquiry into environmental infrastructure for growing populations. Parliament of Victoria
33. Huang S, Wang S, Gan Y et al (2024) Widespread global exacerbation of extreme drought induced by urbanization. Nature Cities 1:597–609. https://doi.org/10.1038/s44284-024-00102-z
34. Richards DR, Thompson BS (2019) Urban ecosystems: A new frontier for payments for ecosystem services. People Nat 1:249–261. https://doi.org/10.1002/pan3.20
35. Clune S, Morrissey J, Moore T (2012) Size matters: House size and thermal efficiency as policy strategies to reduce net emissions of new developments. Energy Policy 48:657–667. https://doi.org/10.1016/j.enpol.2012.05.072
36. Selinske MJ, Howard N, Fitzsimons JA, et al (2022) "Splitting the bill" for conservation: Perceptions and uptake of financial incentives by landholders managing privately protected areas. Conserv Sci Pract 4:n/a. https://doi.org/10.1111/csp2.12660
37. Victoria State Government (2017) Apartment Design Guidelines for Victoria. https://www.planning.vic.gov.au/__data/assets/pdf_file/0030/80994/Apartment-Design-Guidelines-for-Victoria_August-2017.pdf
38. Government of Western Australia (2019) State Planning Policy 7.3 Residential Design Codes, Volume 2—Apartments
39. Pandit R, Polyakov M, Tapsuwan S, Moran T (2013) The effect of street trees on property value in Perth, Western Australia. Landsc Urban Plan 110:134–142. https://doi.org/10.1016/j.landurbplan.2012.11.001
40. Buxton M, Butt A (2020) The future of the fringe: The crisis in peri-urban planning. CSIRO Publishing
41. Kalliolevo H, Gordon A, Sharma R, et al (2021) Biodiversity offsetting can relocate nature away from people: An empirical case study in Western Australia. Conserv Sci Pract 3. https://doi.org/10.1111/csp2.512
42. Lin BB, Meyers JA, Barnett GB (2019) Establishing priorities for urban green infrastructure research in Australia. Urban Policy Res 37:30–44. https://doi.org/10.1080/08111146.2018.1523054
43. Pakzad P, Osmond P, Corkery L (2017) Developing key sustainability indicators for assessing green infrastructure performance. Procedia Eng 180:146–156. https://doi.org/10.1016/j.proeng.2017.04.174
44. Marshall AJ, Grose MJ, Williams NSG (2019) From little things: more than a third of public green space is road verge. Urban For Urban Green 44:126423. https://doi.org/10.1016/j.ufug.2019.126423
45. Newton PW, Newman PWG, Glackin S, Thomson G (2022) Climate resilience and regeneration: How precincts can adapt to and mitigate climate change. Greening the greyfields. Palgrave Macmillan, Singapore, pp 105–120
46. Dovey K, Woodcock I, Pike L (2015) Intensifying Melbourne: Transit-oriented urban design for resilient urban futures. Planning News 41:10–11
47. Moore GM (2021) Connectivity of public open space: Its meaning for different functions. J Urban Des (Abingdon) 26:279–295. https://doi.org/10.1080/13574809.2020.1801340
48. Bolleter J, Ramalho CE (2019) Greenspace-oriented development: Reconciling urban density and nature in suburban cities, 1st ed. Springer International Publishing AG

49. Kirkpatrick JB, Davison A, Daniels GD (2012) Resident attitudes towards trees influence the planting and removal of different types of trees in eastern Australian cities. Landsc Urban Plan 107:147–158. https://doi.org/10.1016/j.landurbplan.2012.05.015
50. Pearce L, Kirkpatrick J, Davison A (2013) Using size class distributions of species to deduce the dynamics of the private urban forest. Arboric Urban For 39. https://doi.org/10.48044/jauf.2013.011
51. Profous GV, Loeb RE (1990) The legal protection of urban trees: A comparative world Survey. Journal of Environmental Law 2:179–194
52. Hurley J, Amati M, Deilami K, et al (2020) Where will all the trees be? The 2020 update of green cover benchmarking in our cities and suburbs. https://www.greenerspacesbetterplaces.com.au/media/163303/wwattb_v13.pdf. Accessed 14 Dec 2023

FSC
www.fsc.org
MIX
Papier aus verantwortungsvollen Quellen
Paper from responsible sources
FSC® C105338

If you have any concerns about our products,
you can contact us on
ProductSafety@springernature.com

In case Publisher is established outside the EU,
the EU authorized representative is:
Springer Nature Customer Service Center GmbH
Europaplatz 3, 69115 Heidelberg, Germany

Printed by Libri Plureos GmbH
in Hamburg, Germany